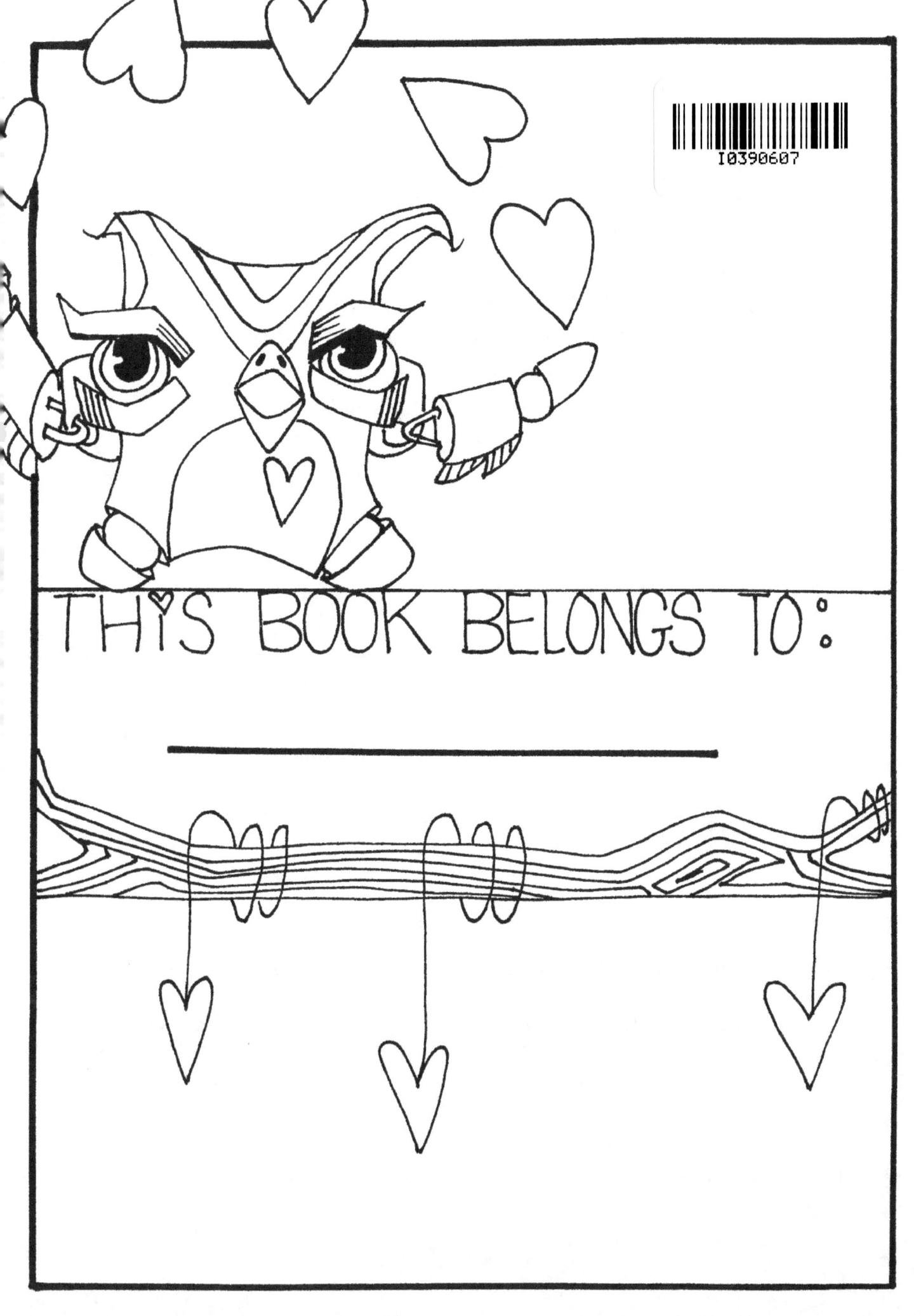

THIS BOOK BELONGS TO:

Thank you for joining me on a journey
into the world of whimsy.
I have created 30 beautifully detailed one of a kind
images for you to enjoy.
With each of their fantastic personalities shining
through, they are waiting for you to
bring them to life!!
Jenny :)

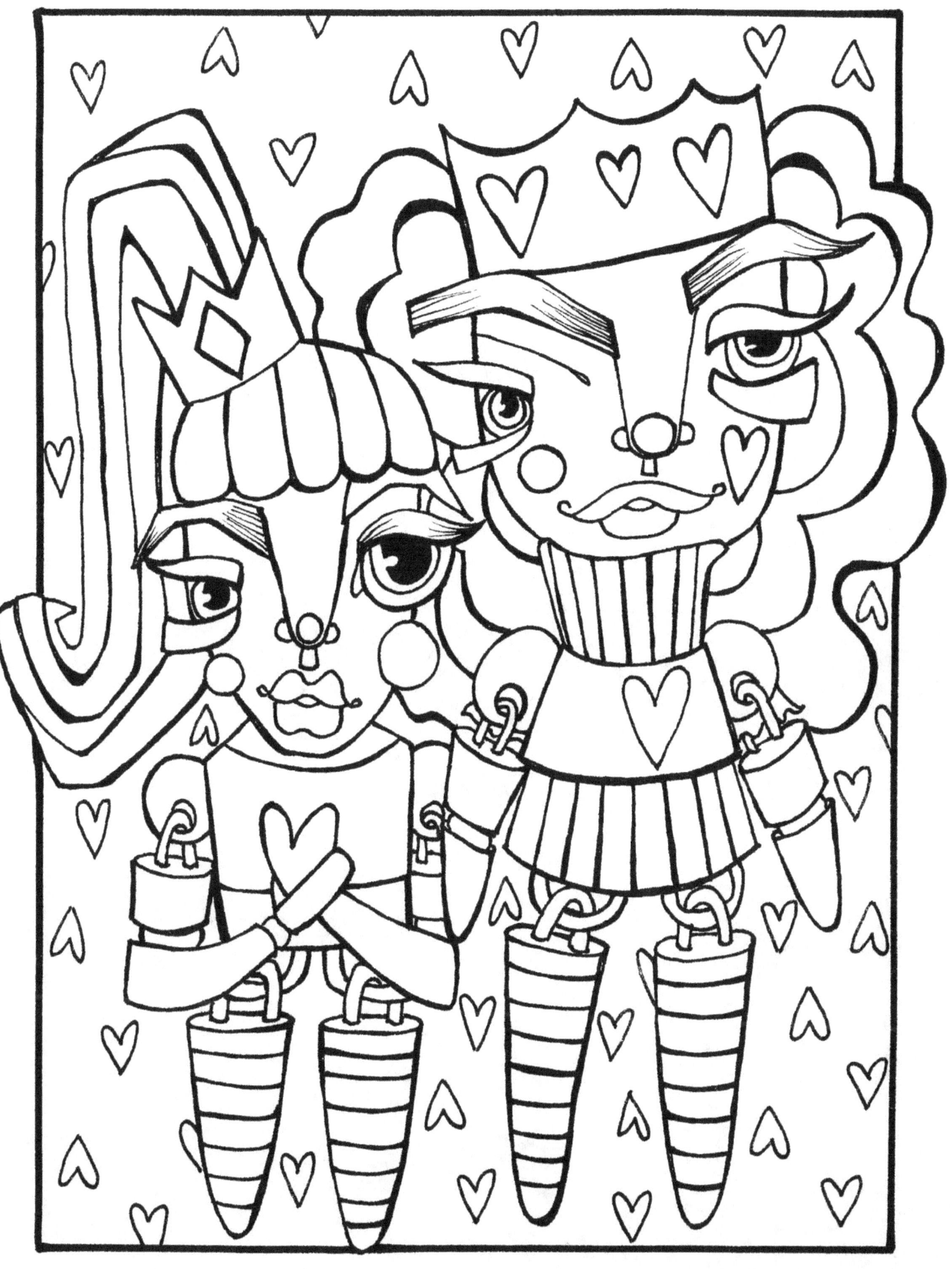

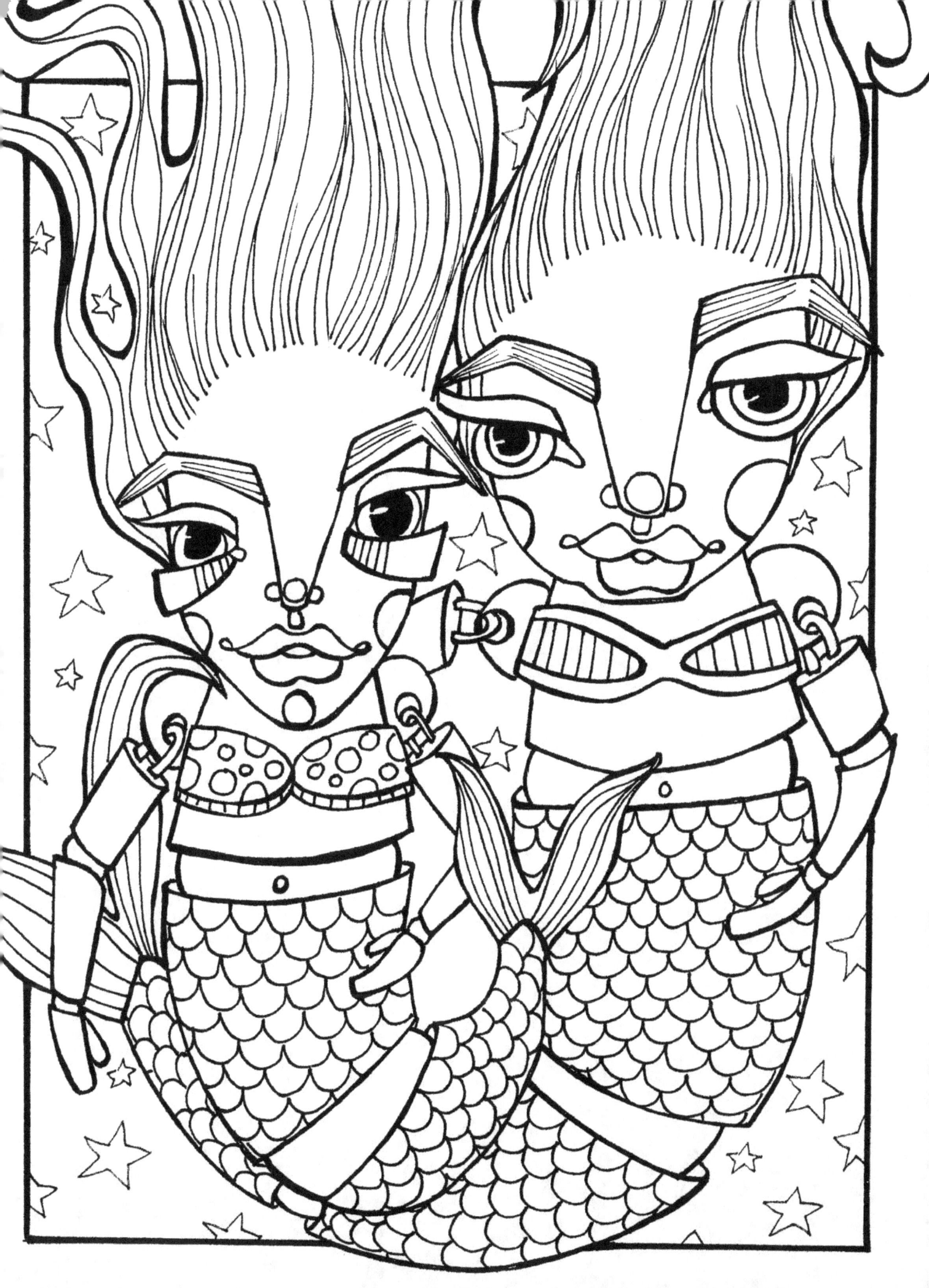

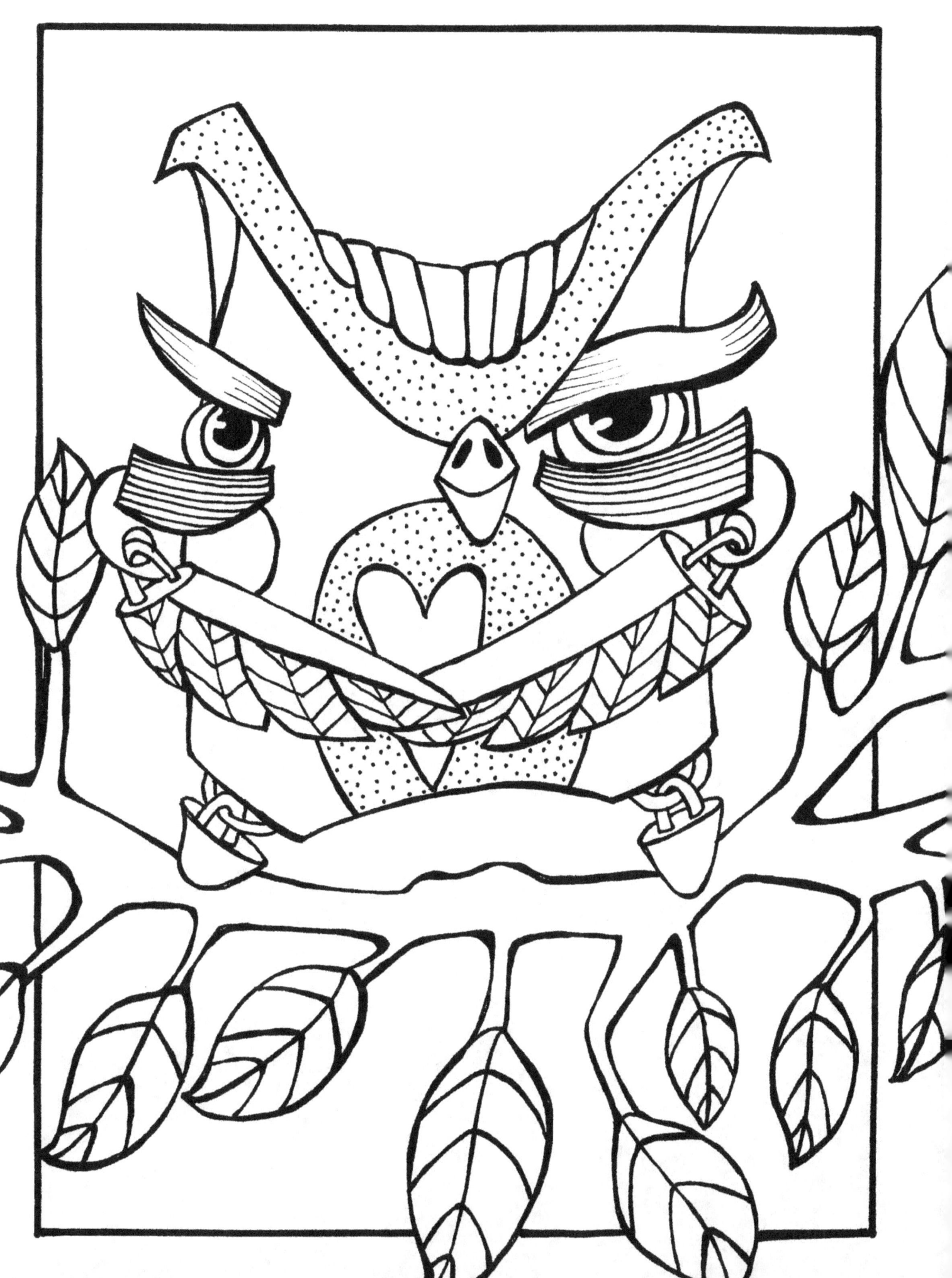

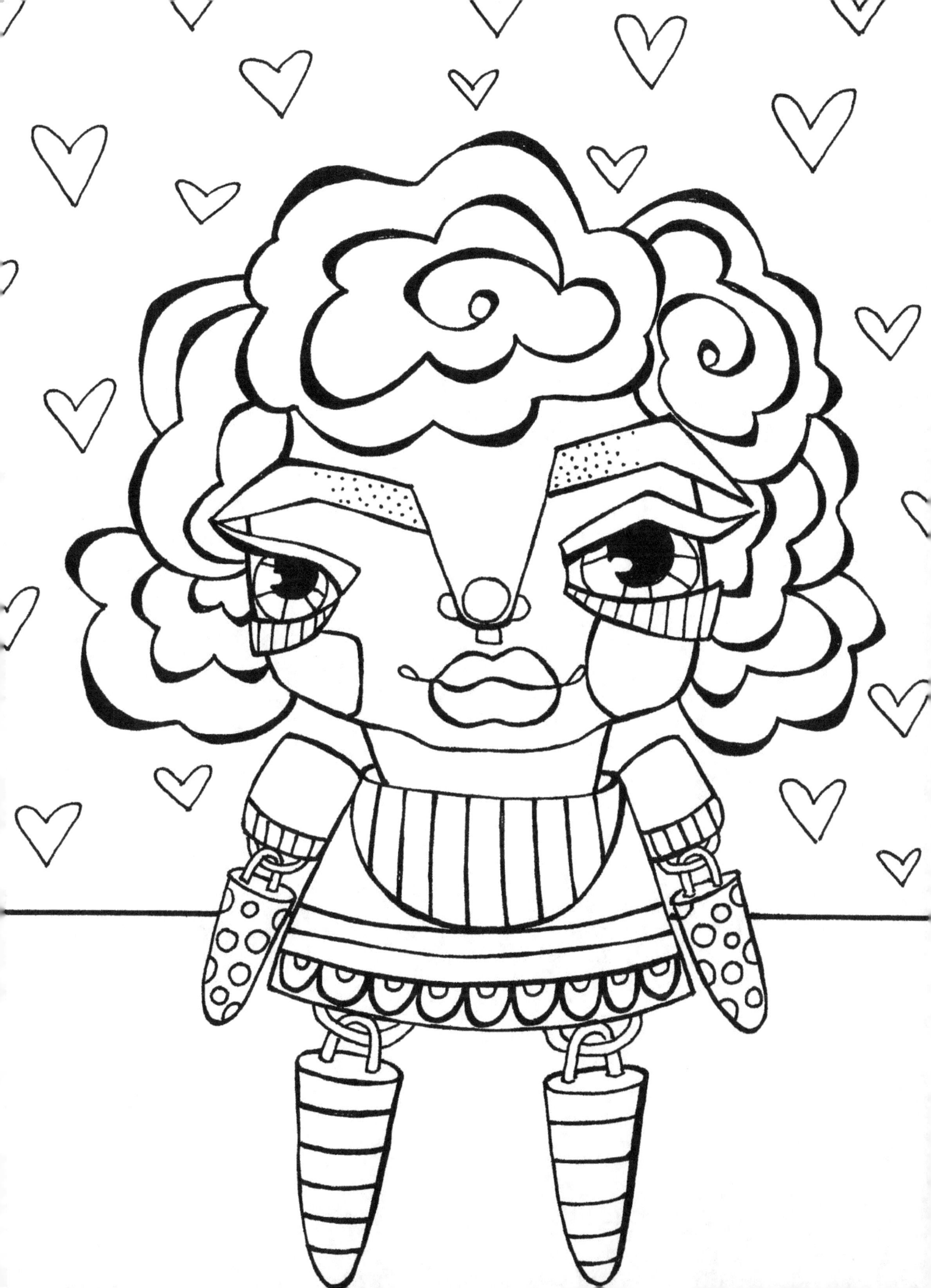

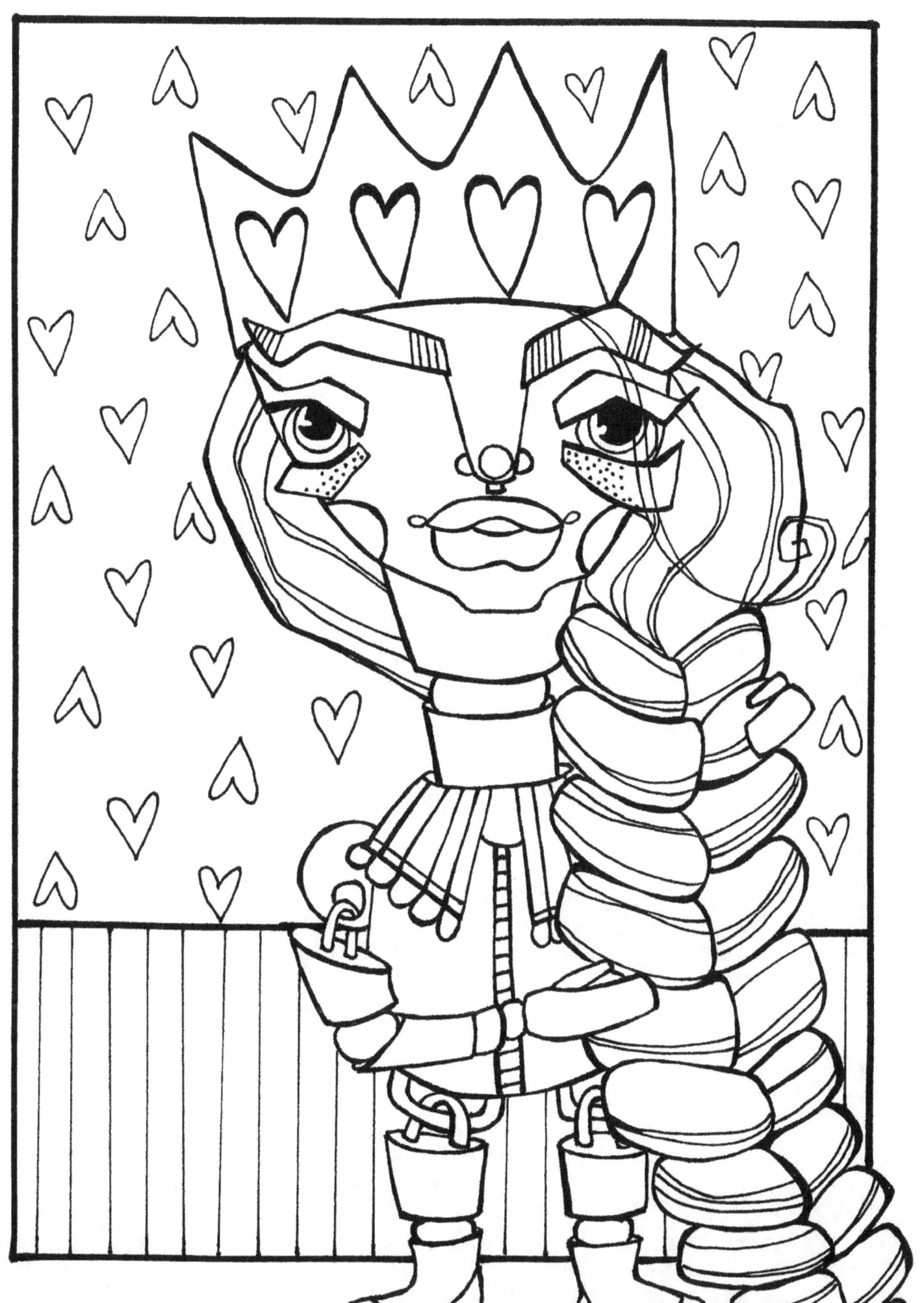

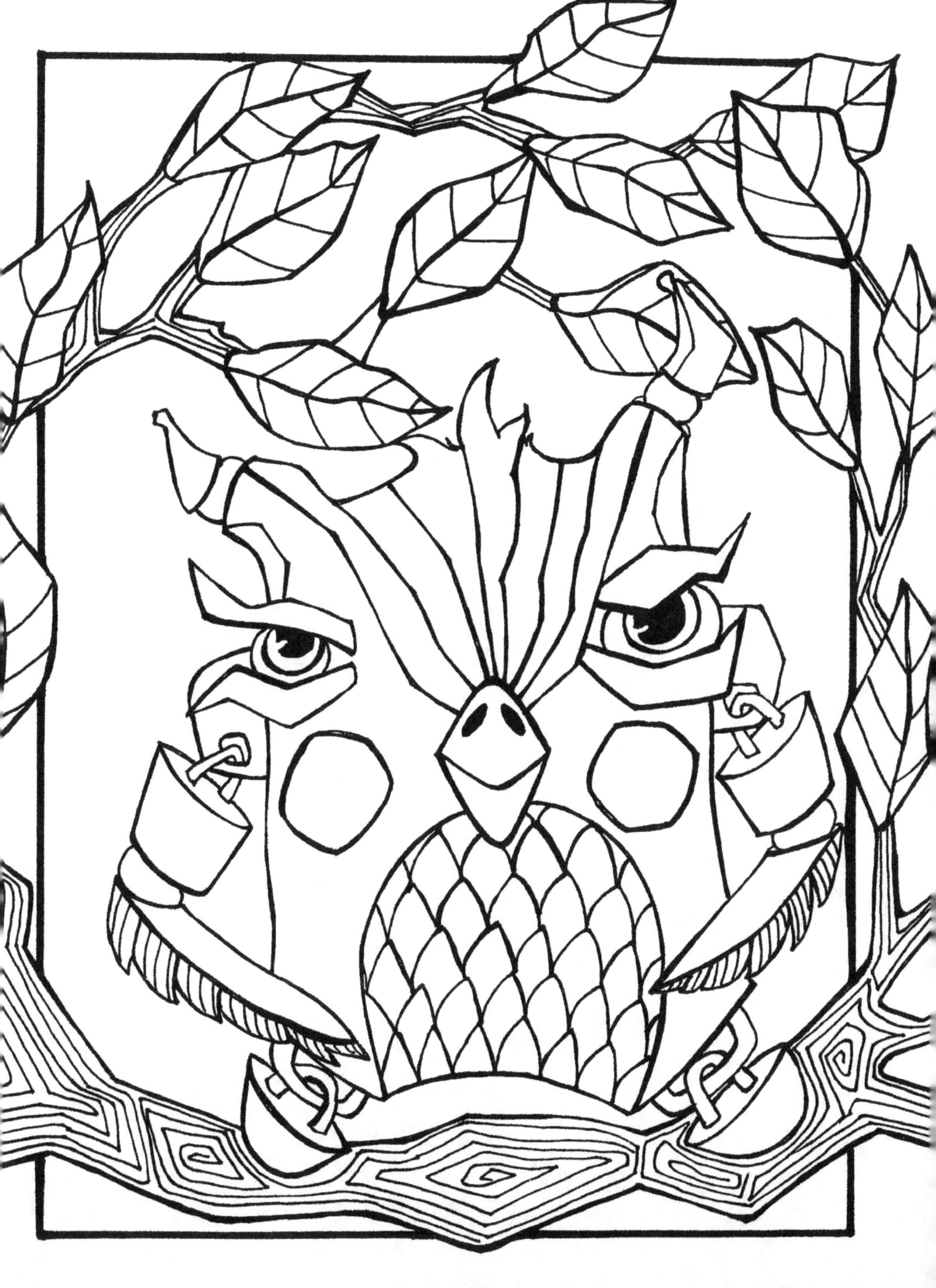

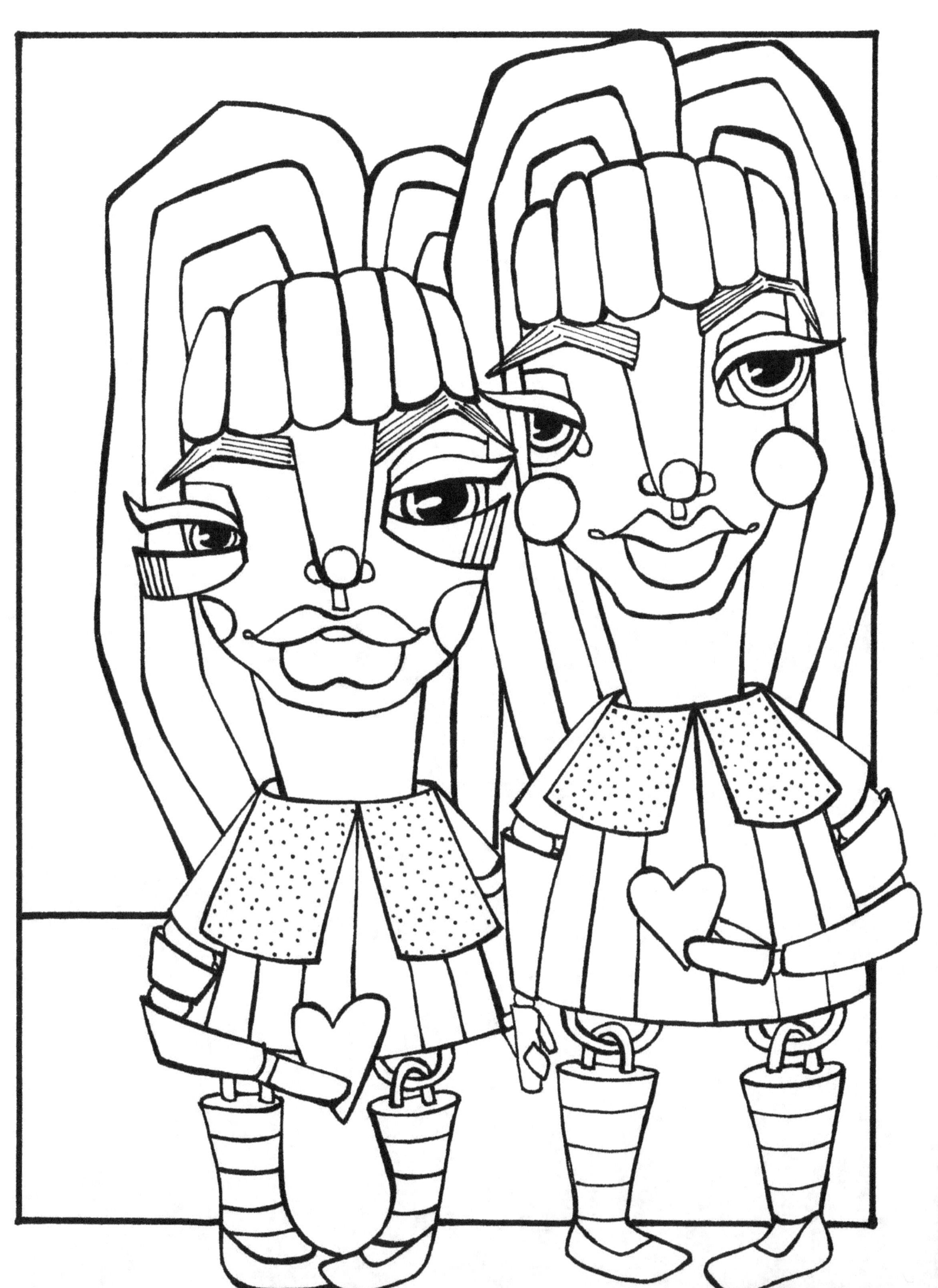

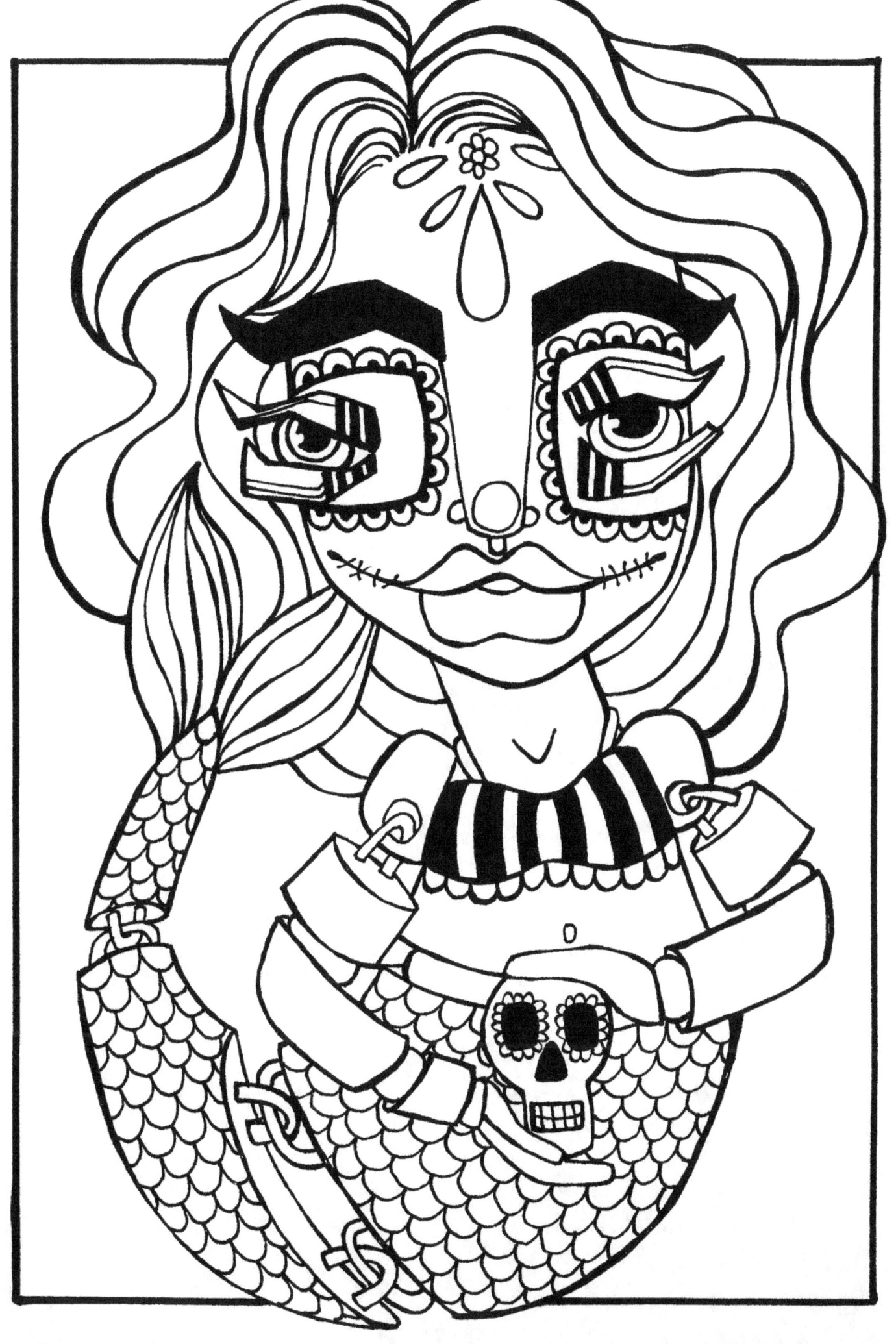

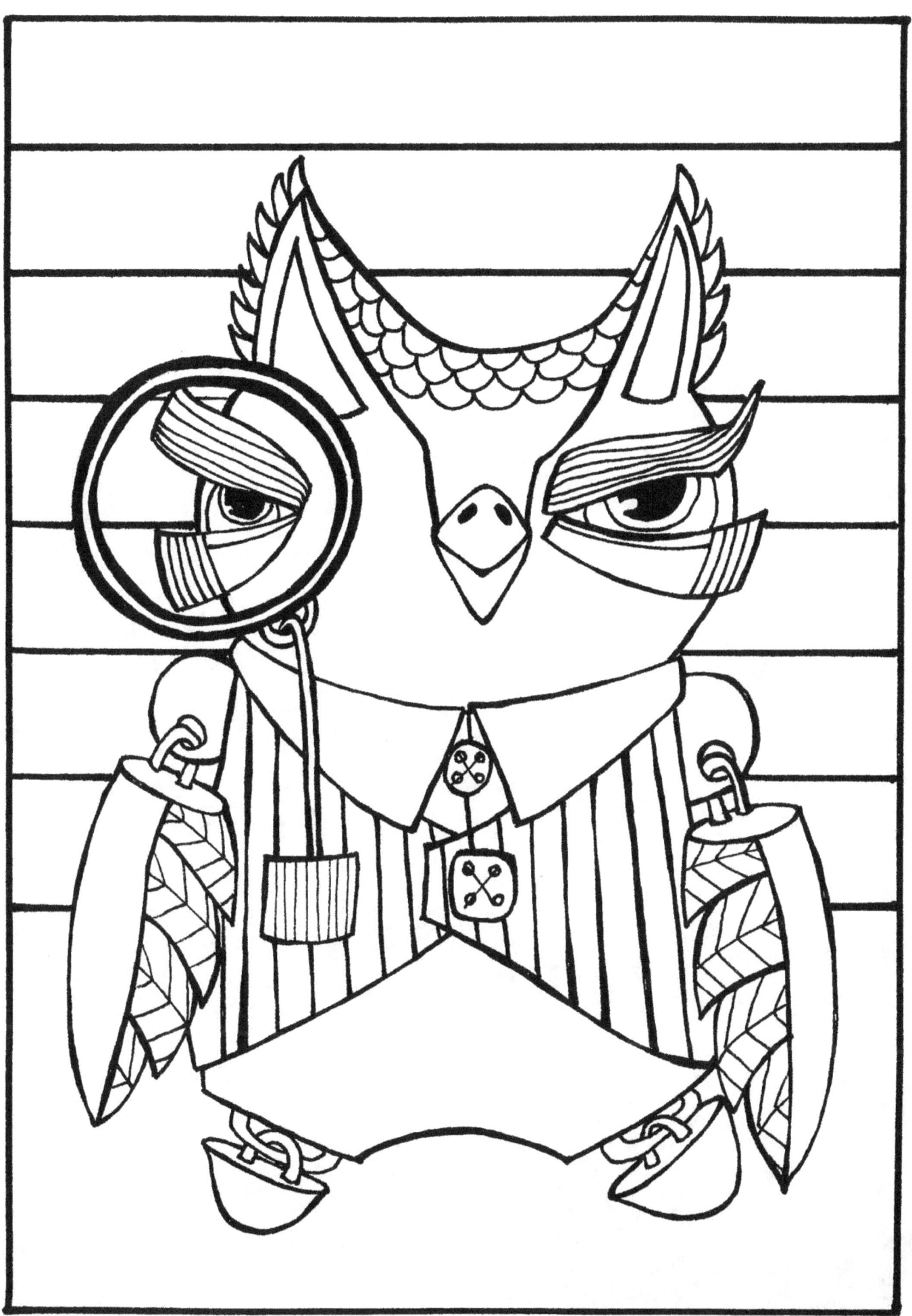

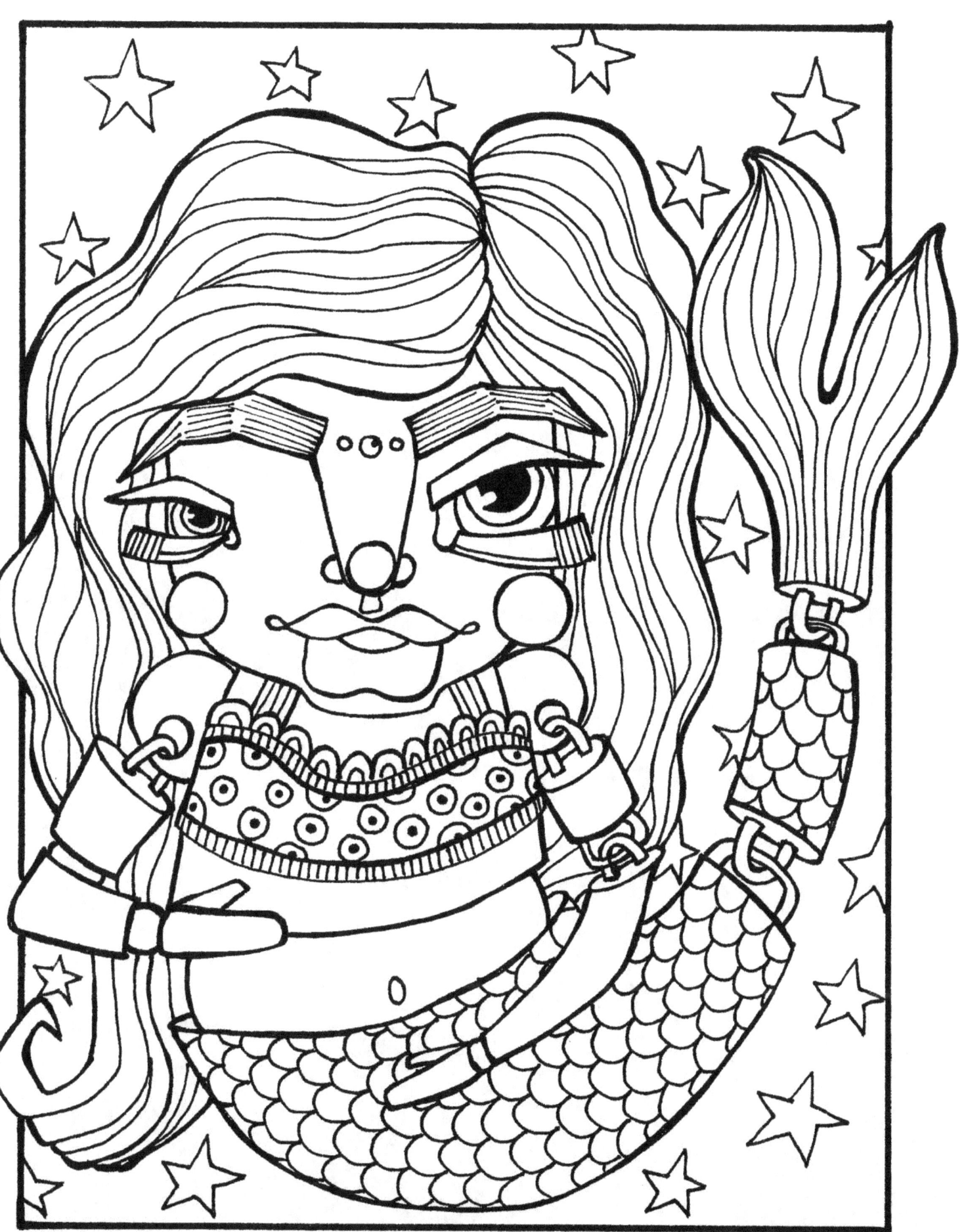

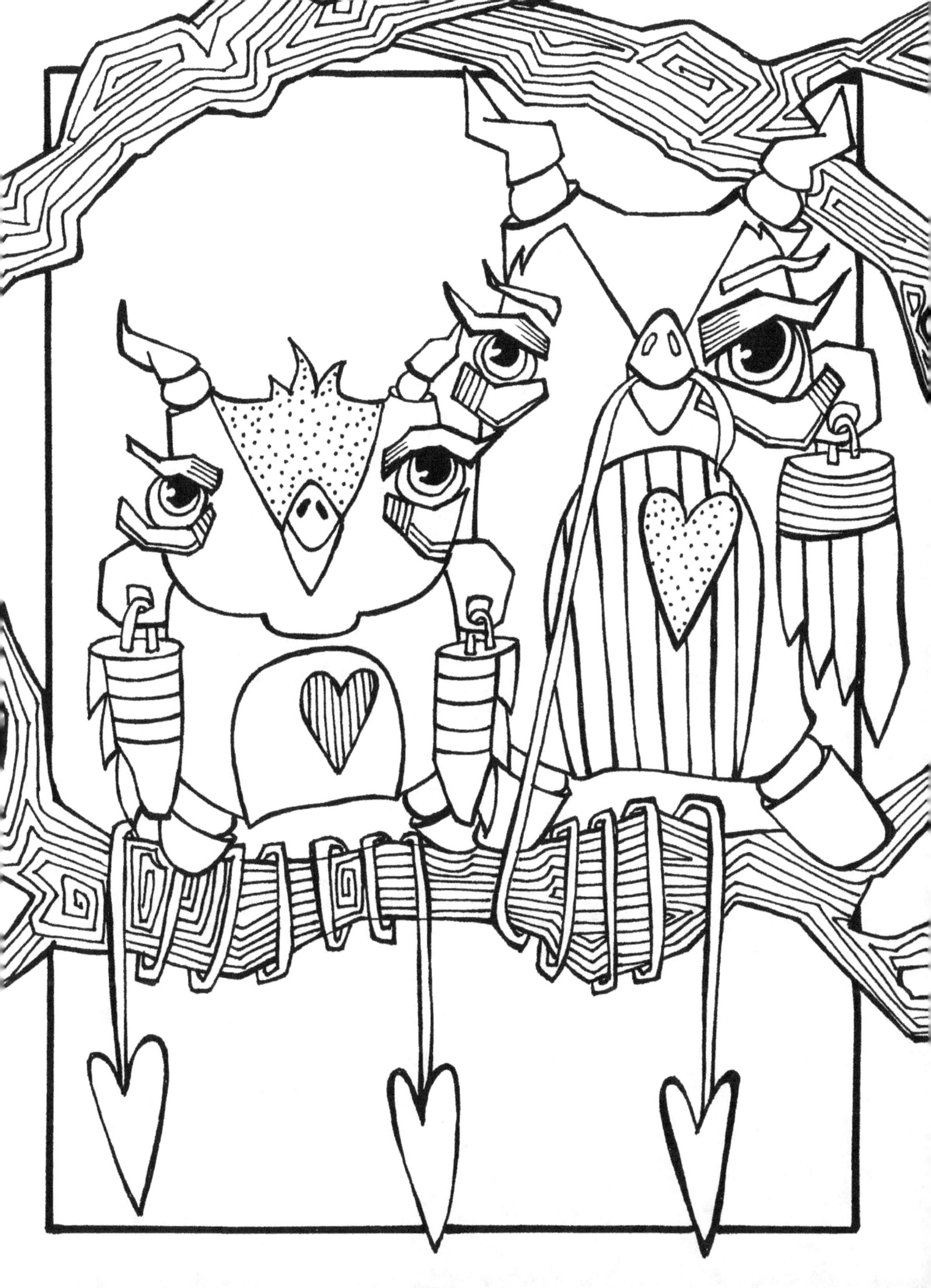

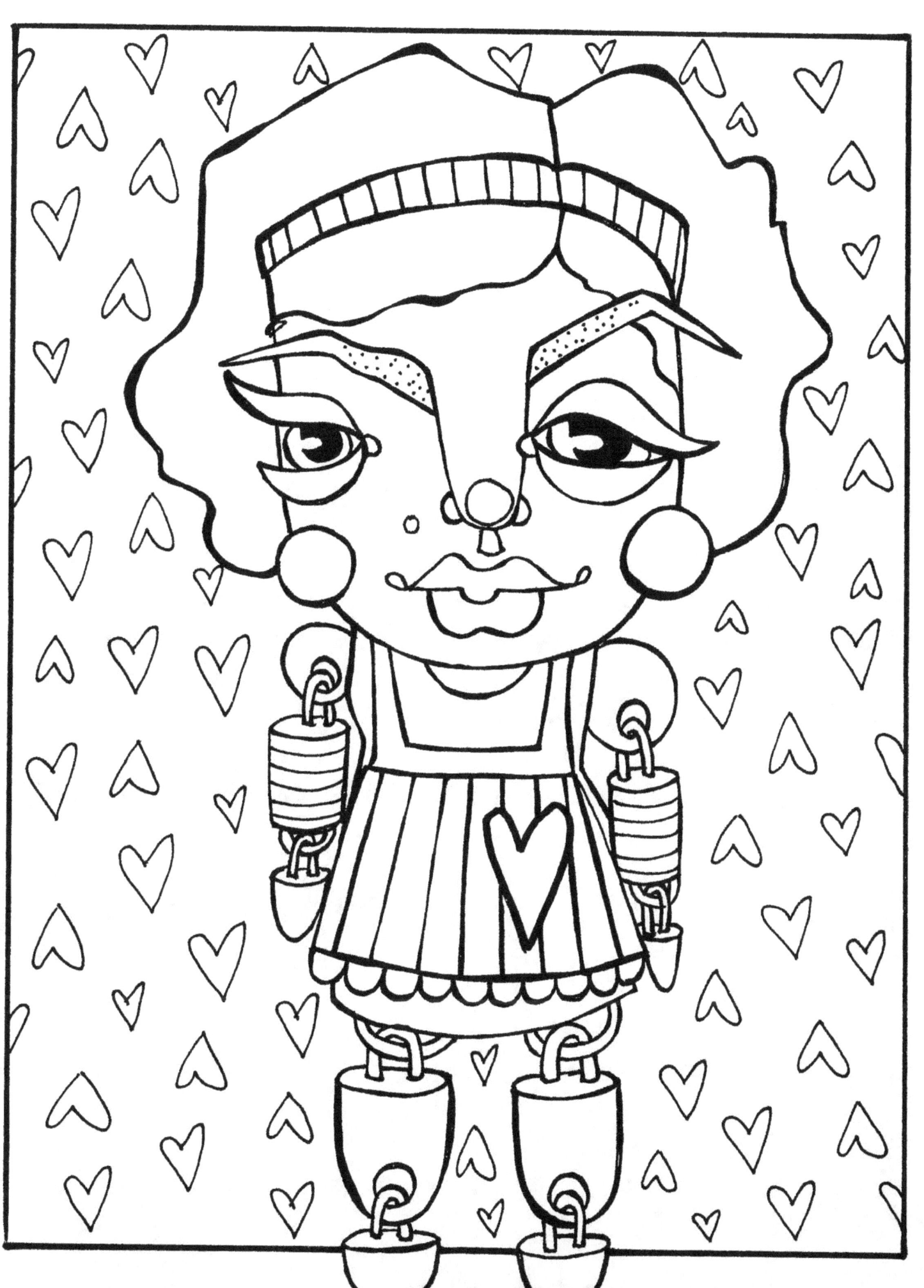

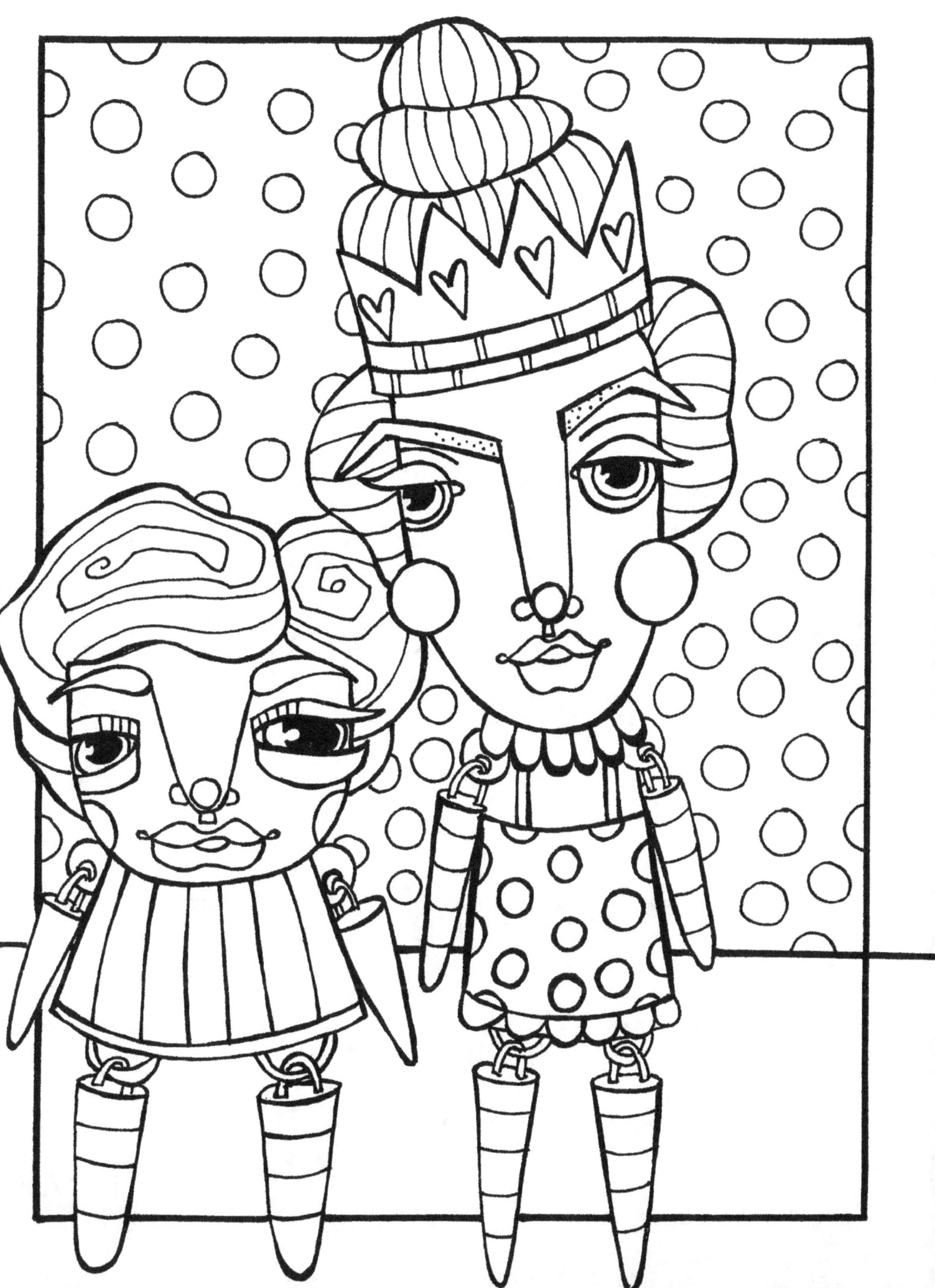

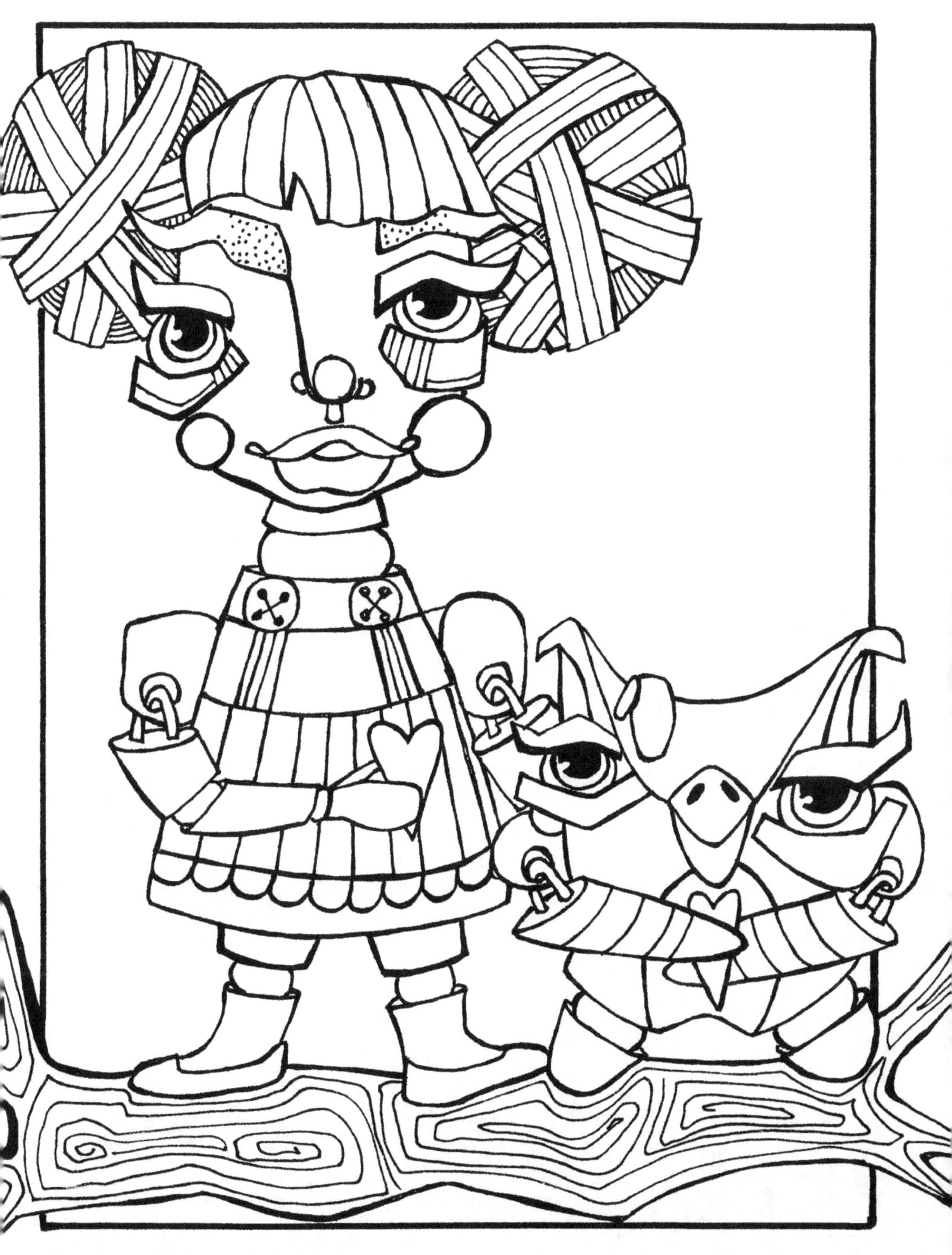

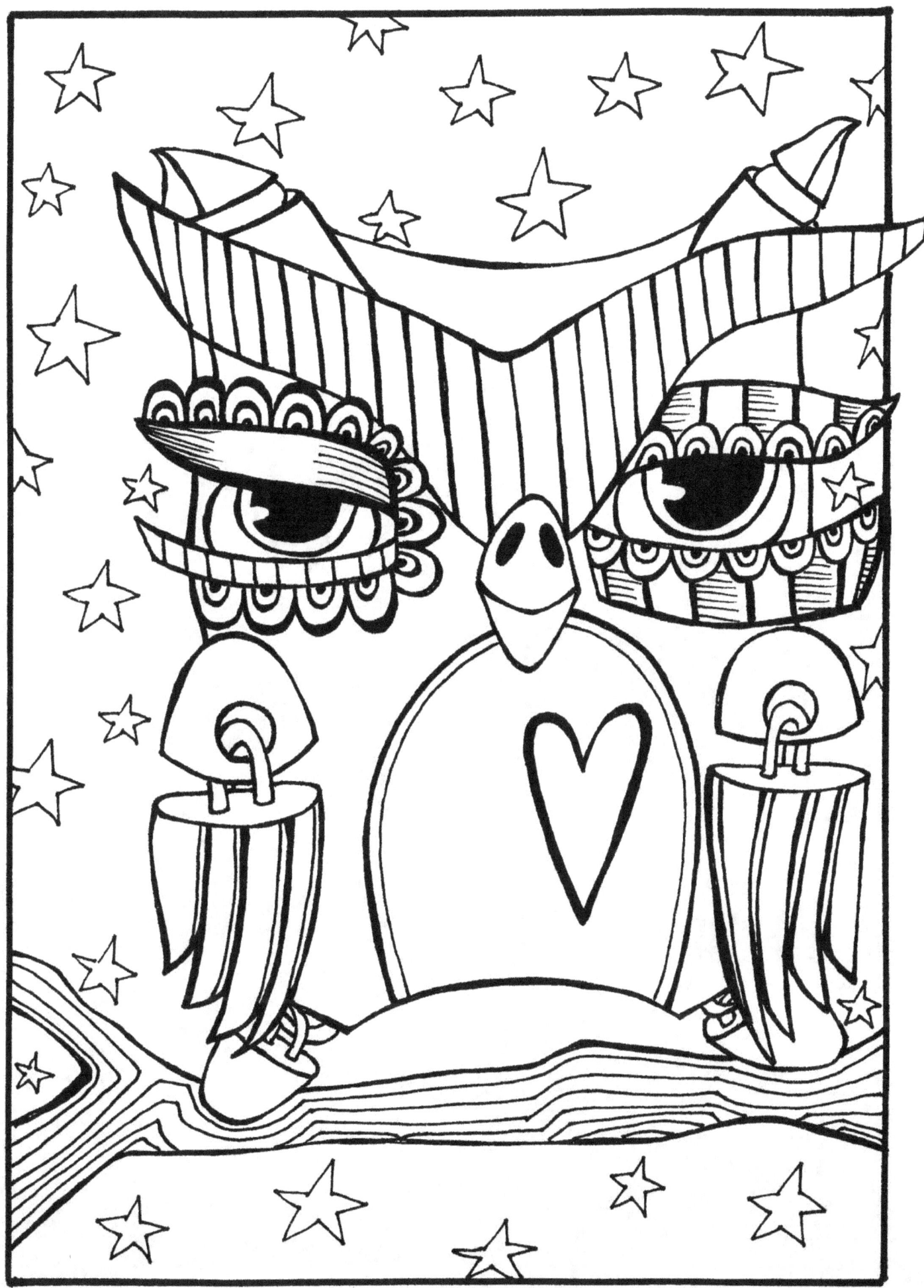

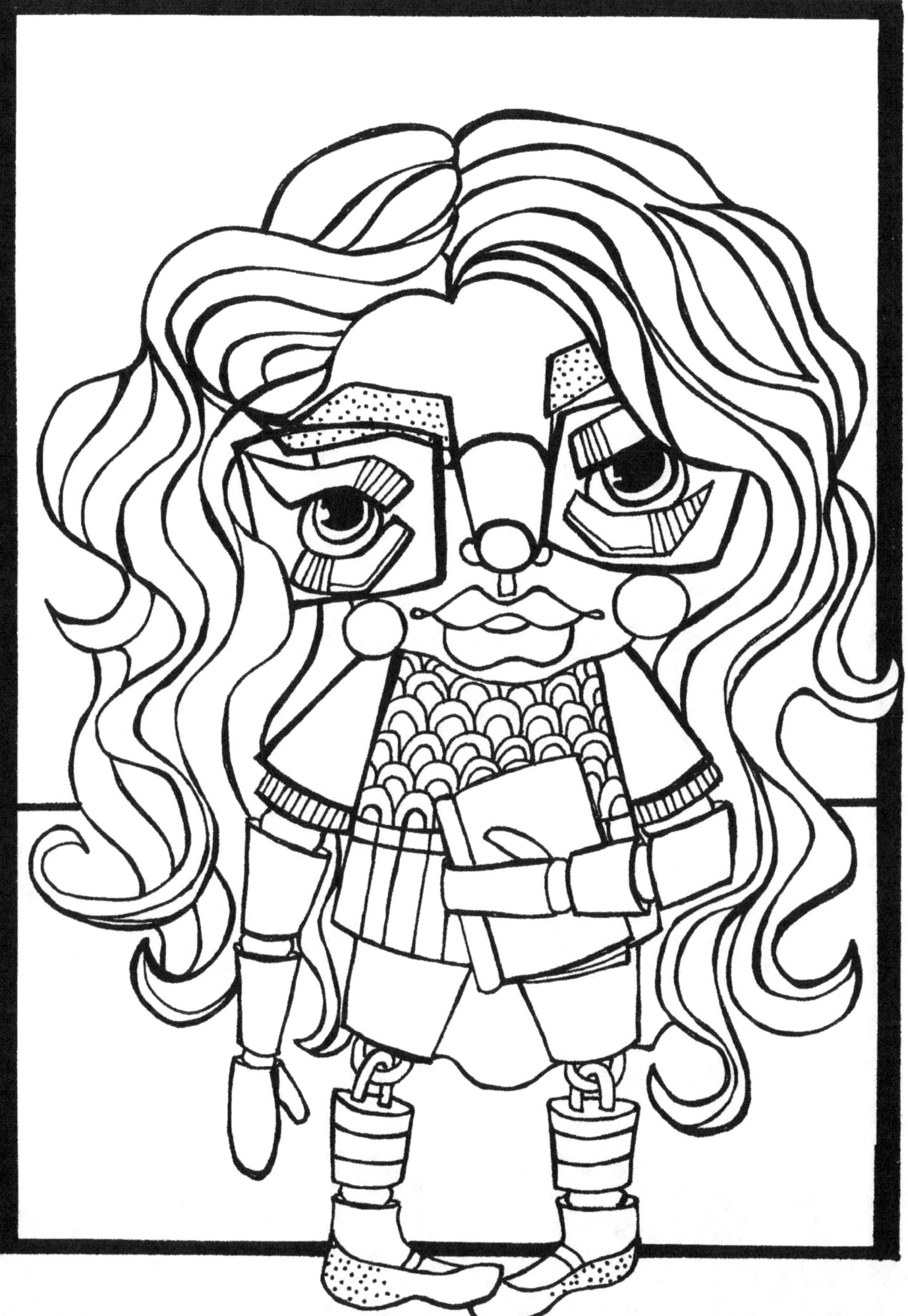

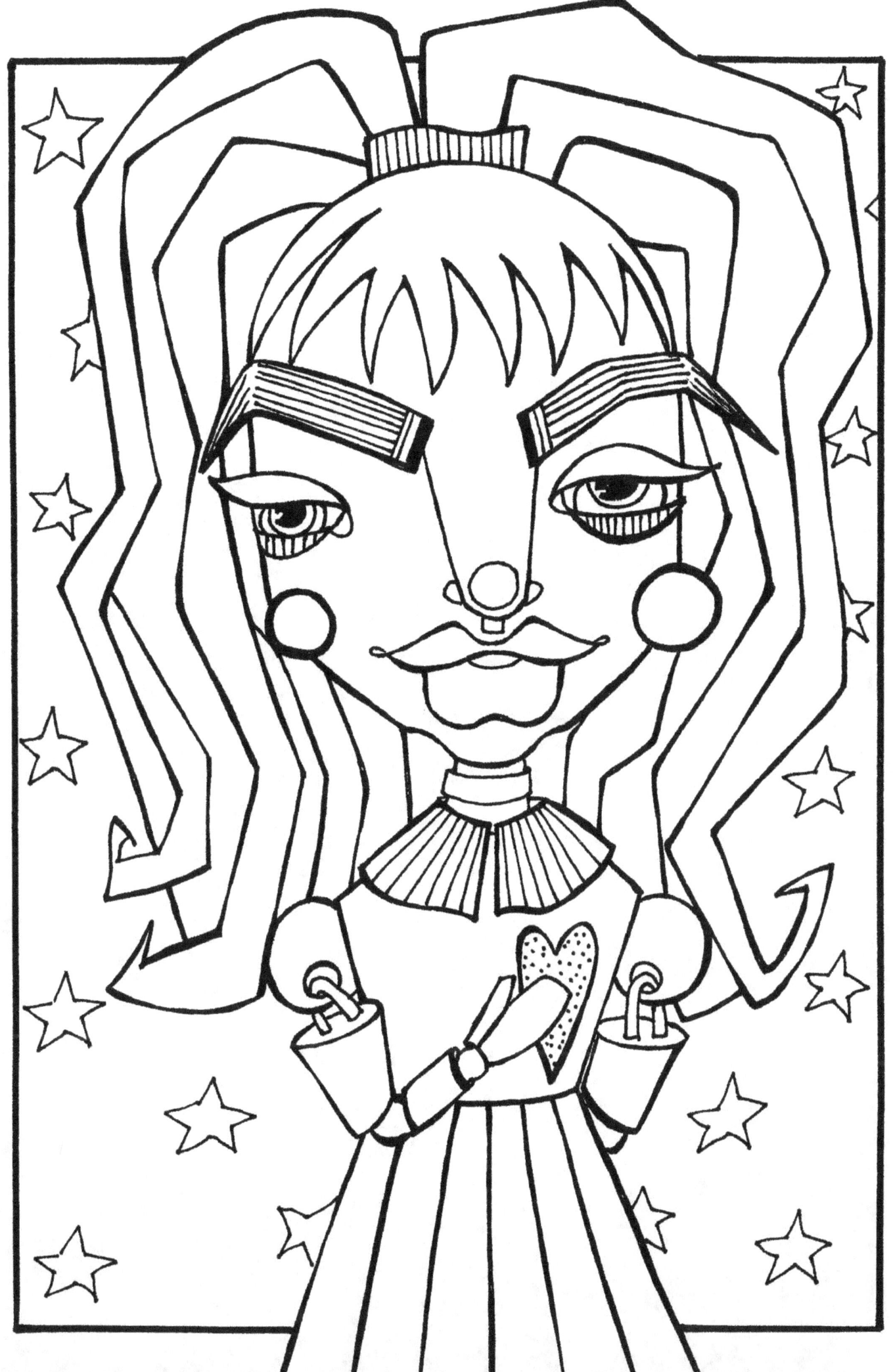

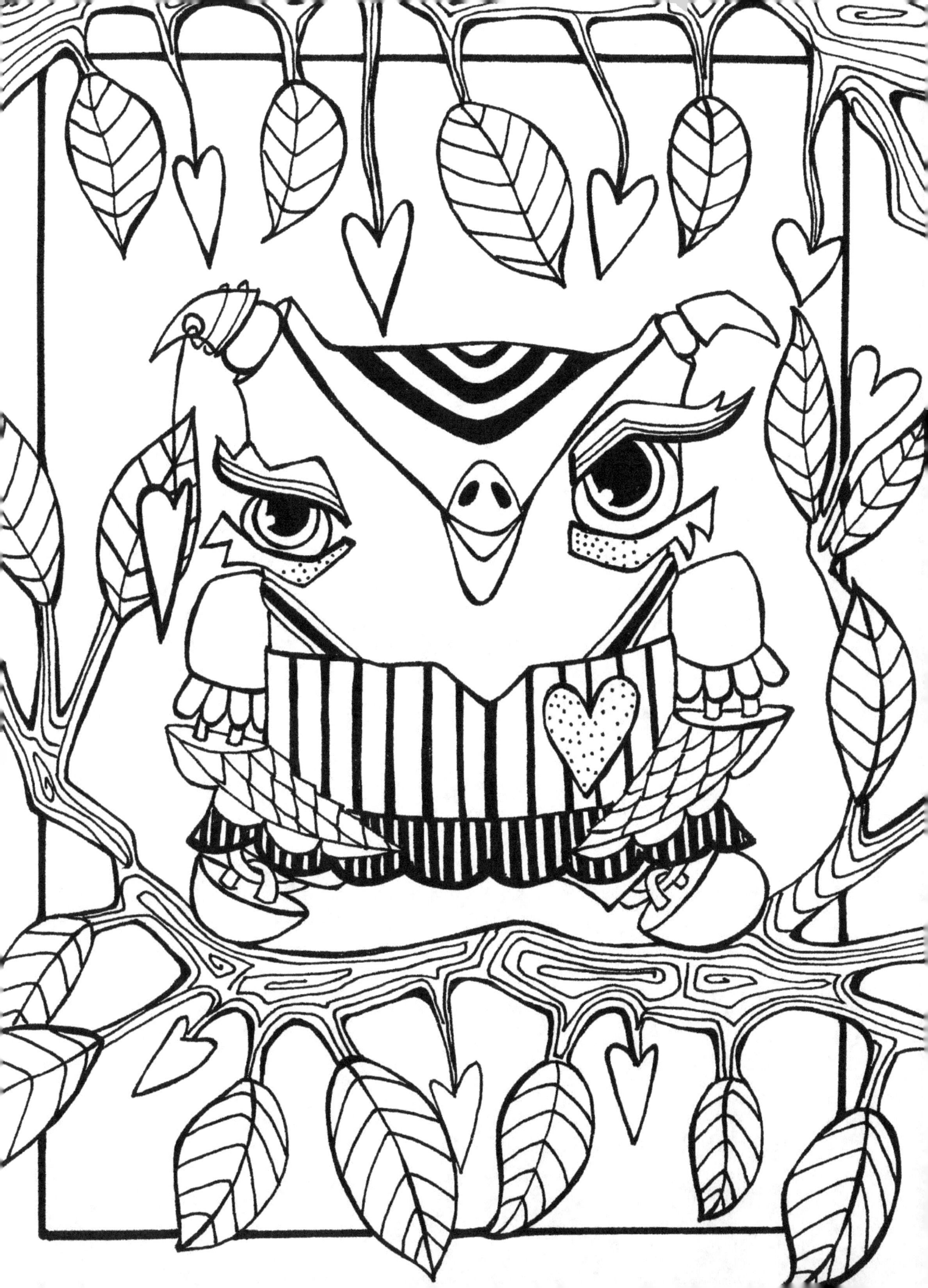

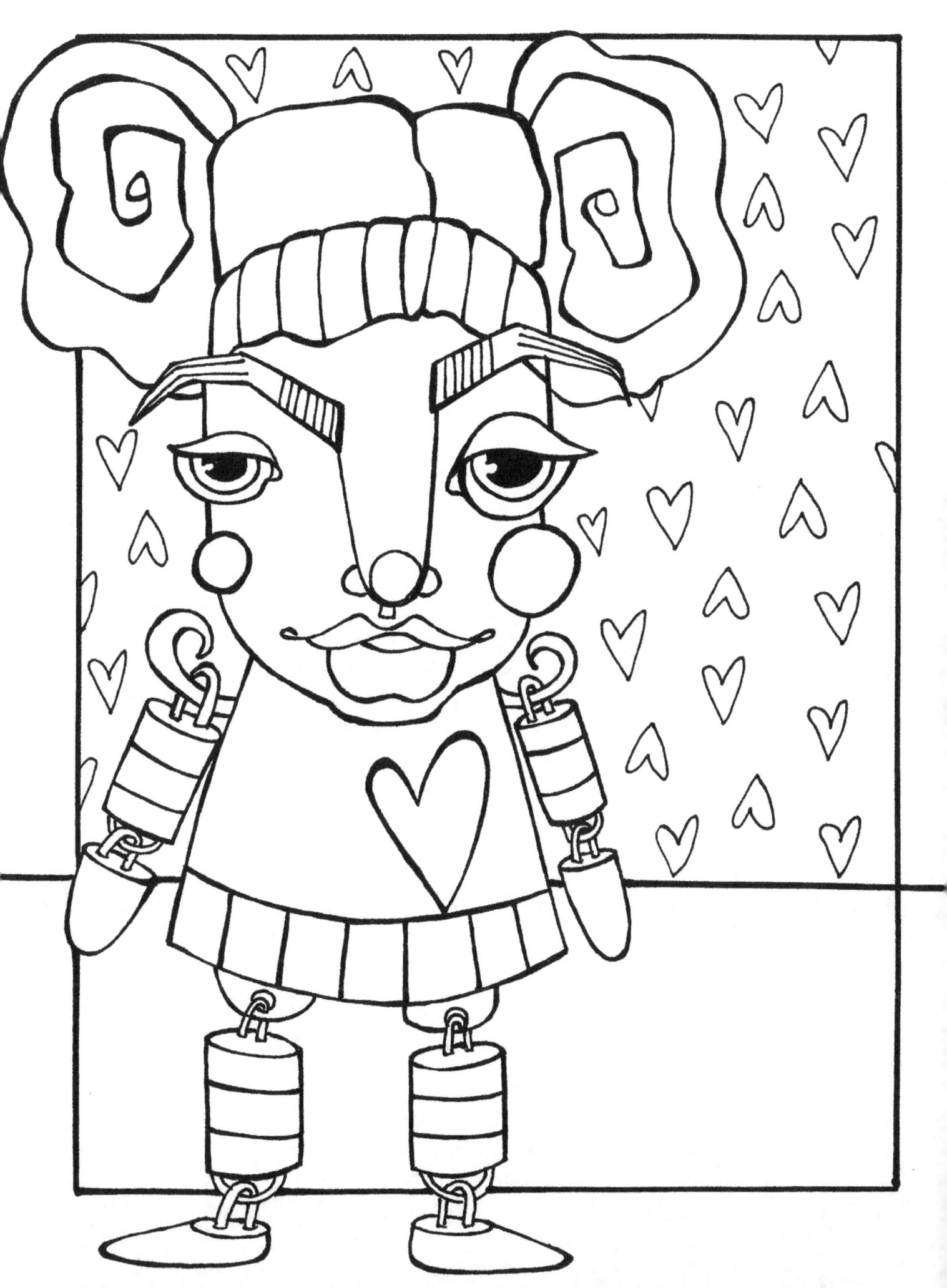

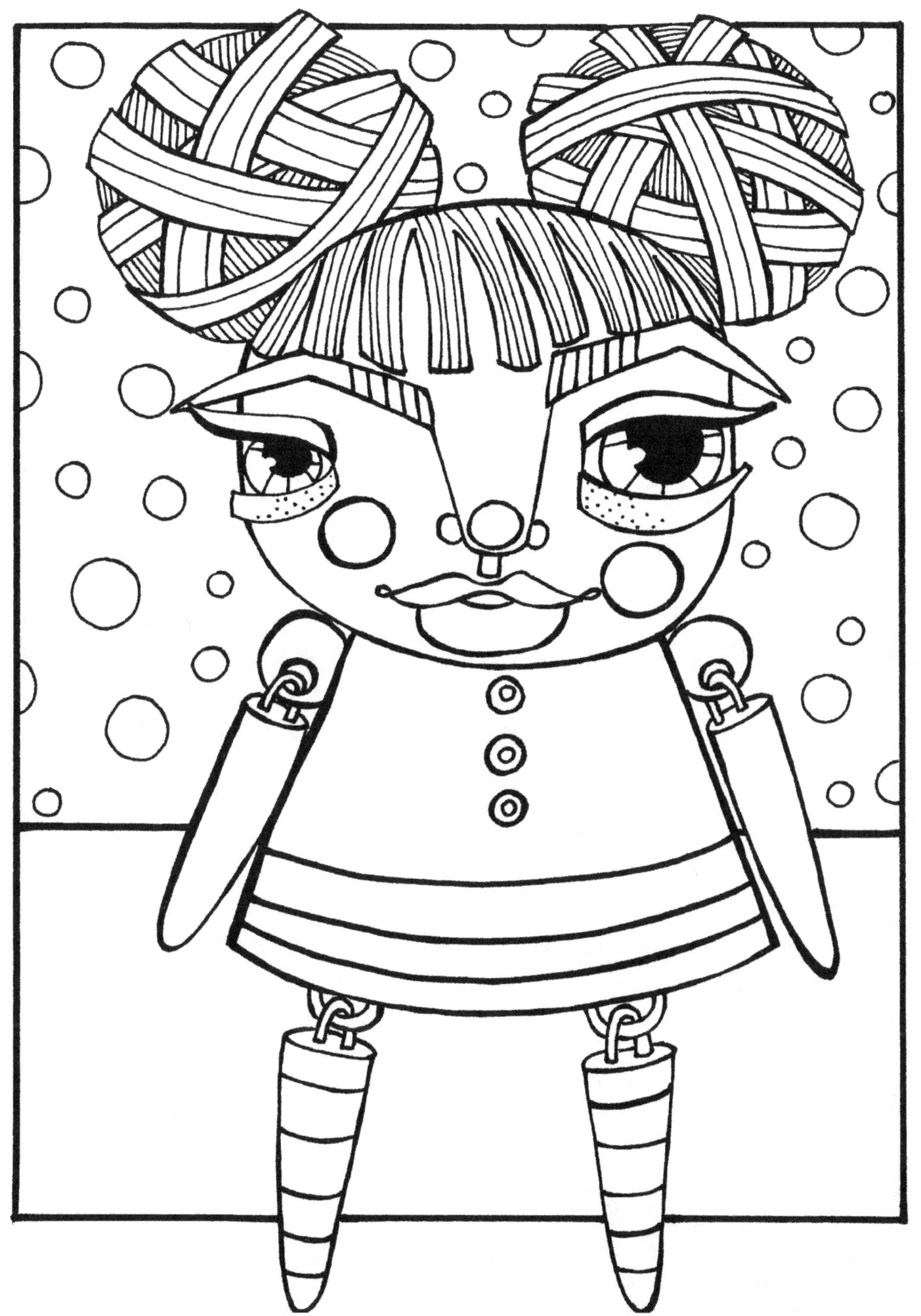

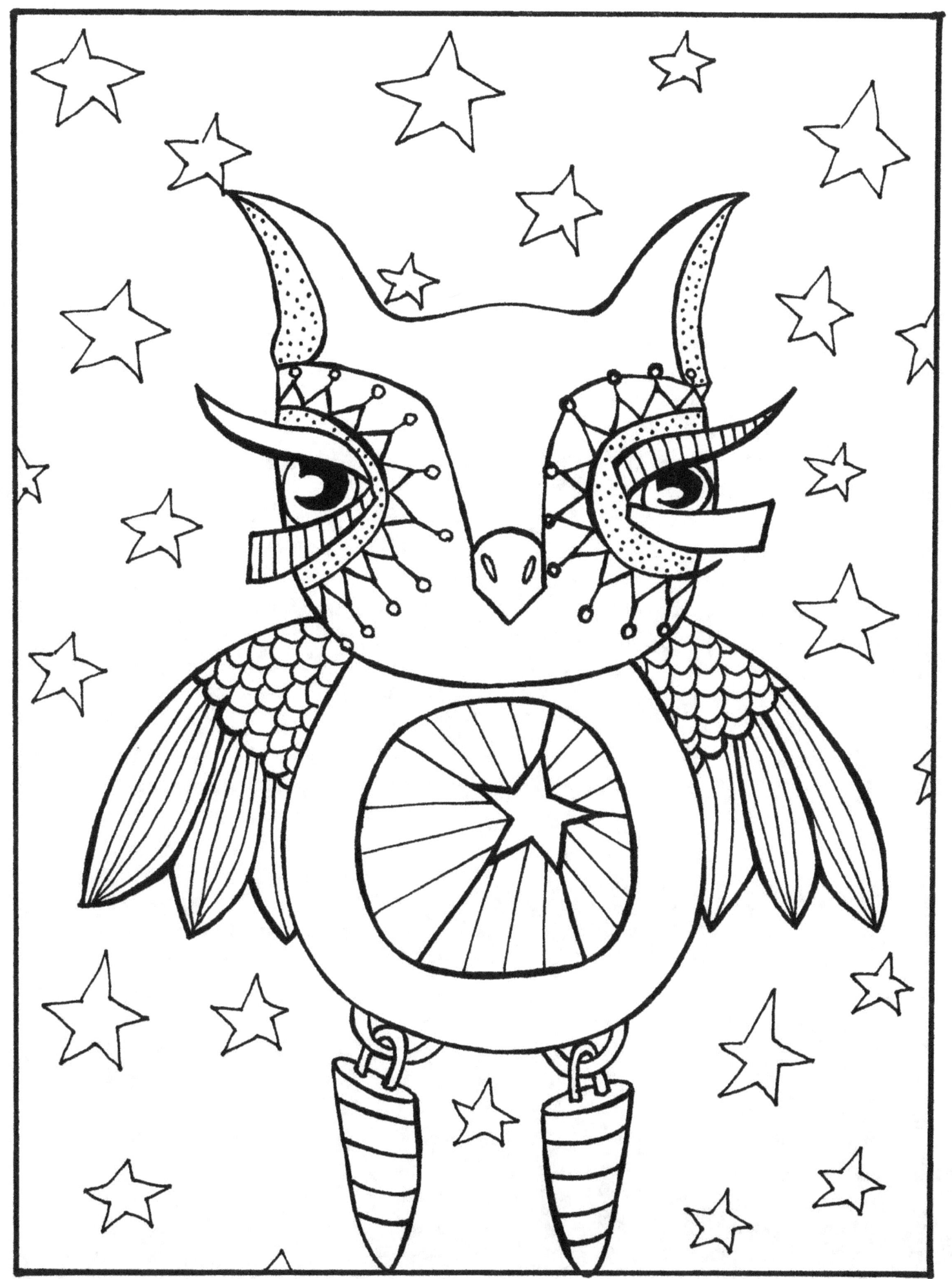

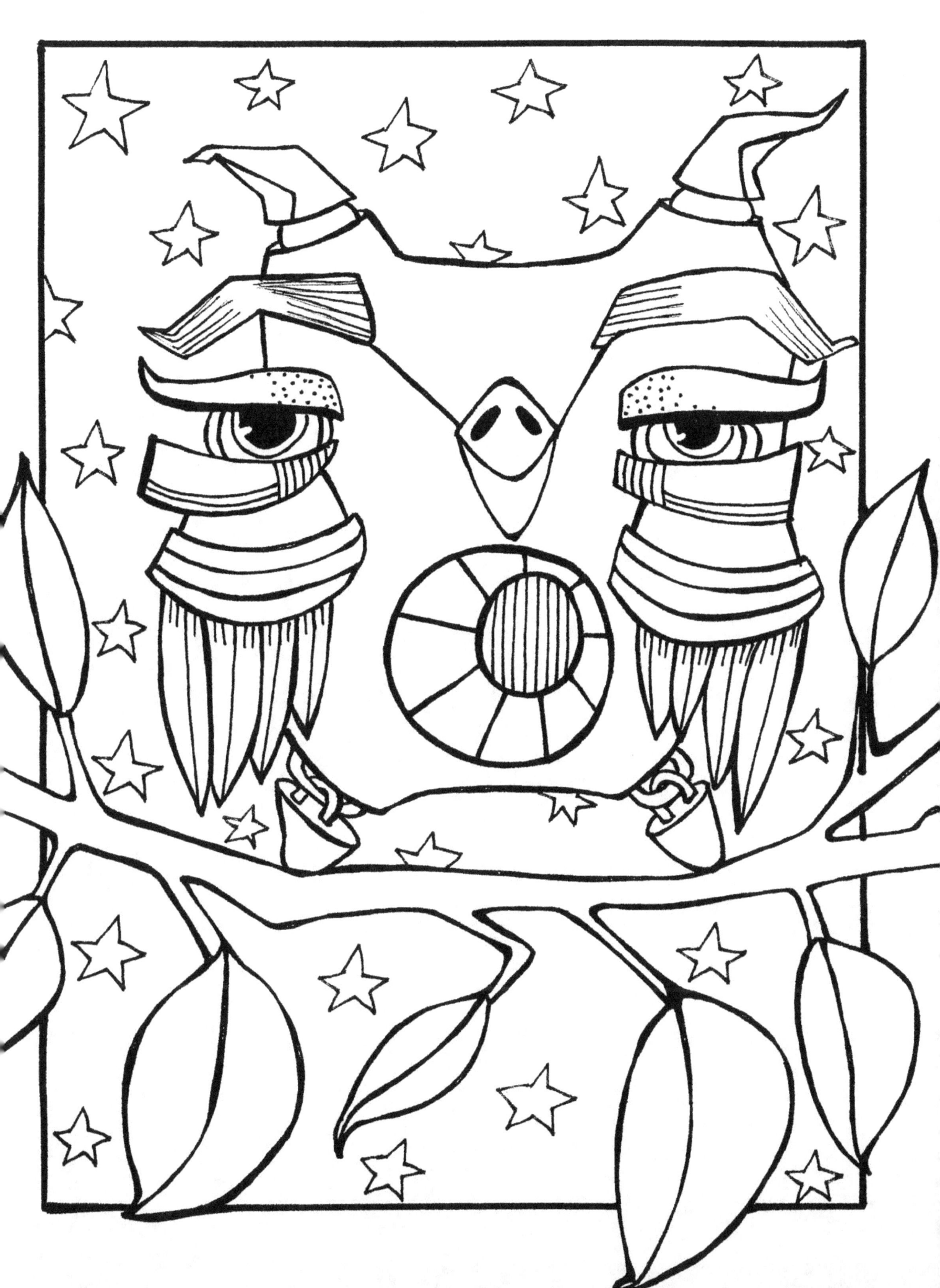

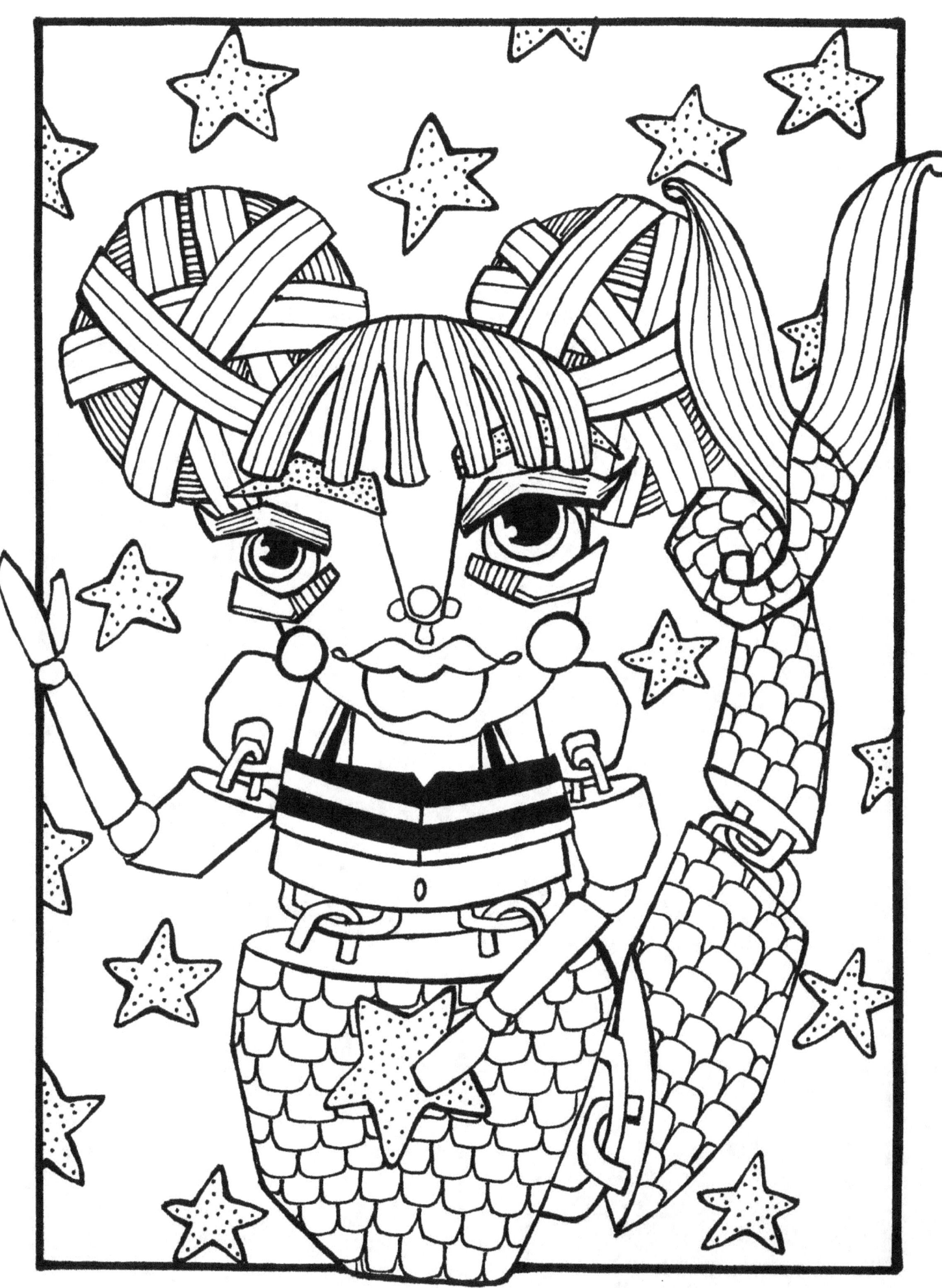

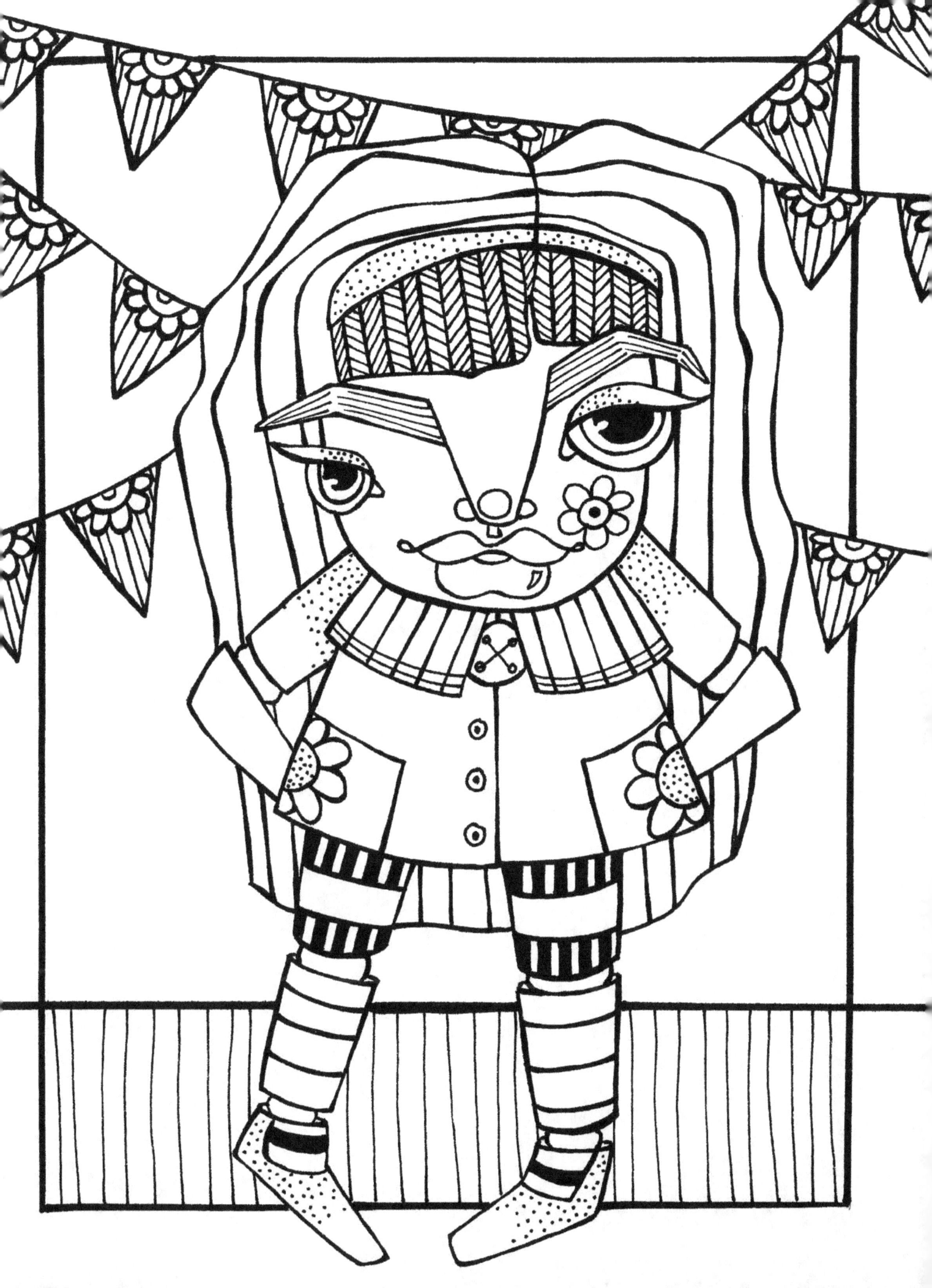

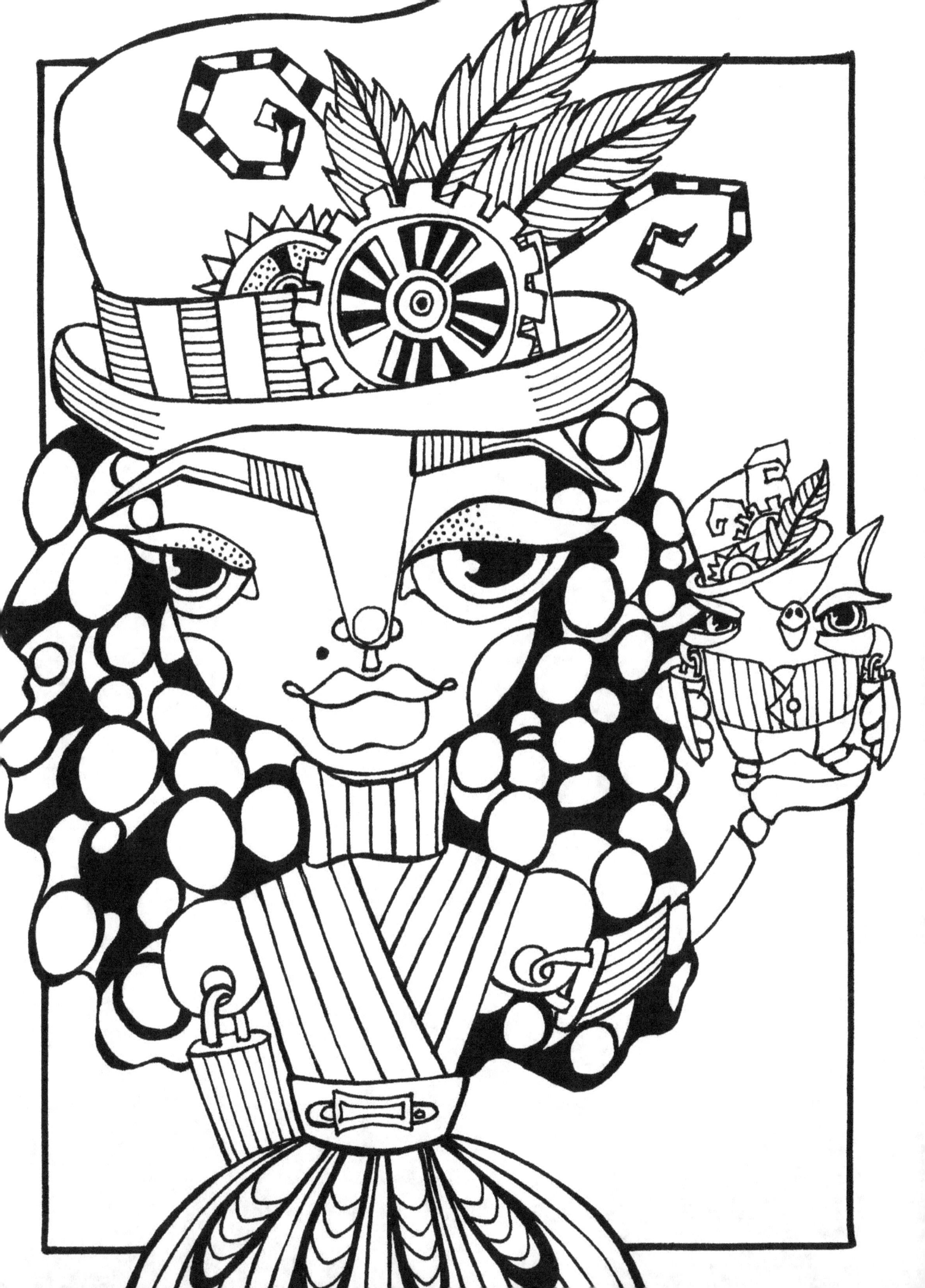

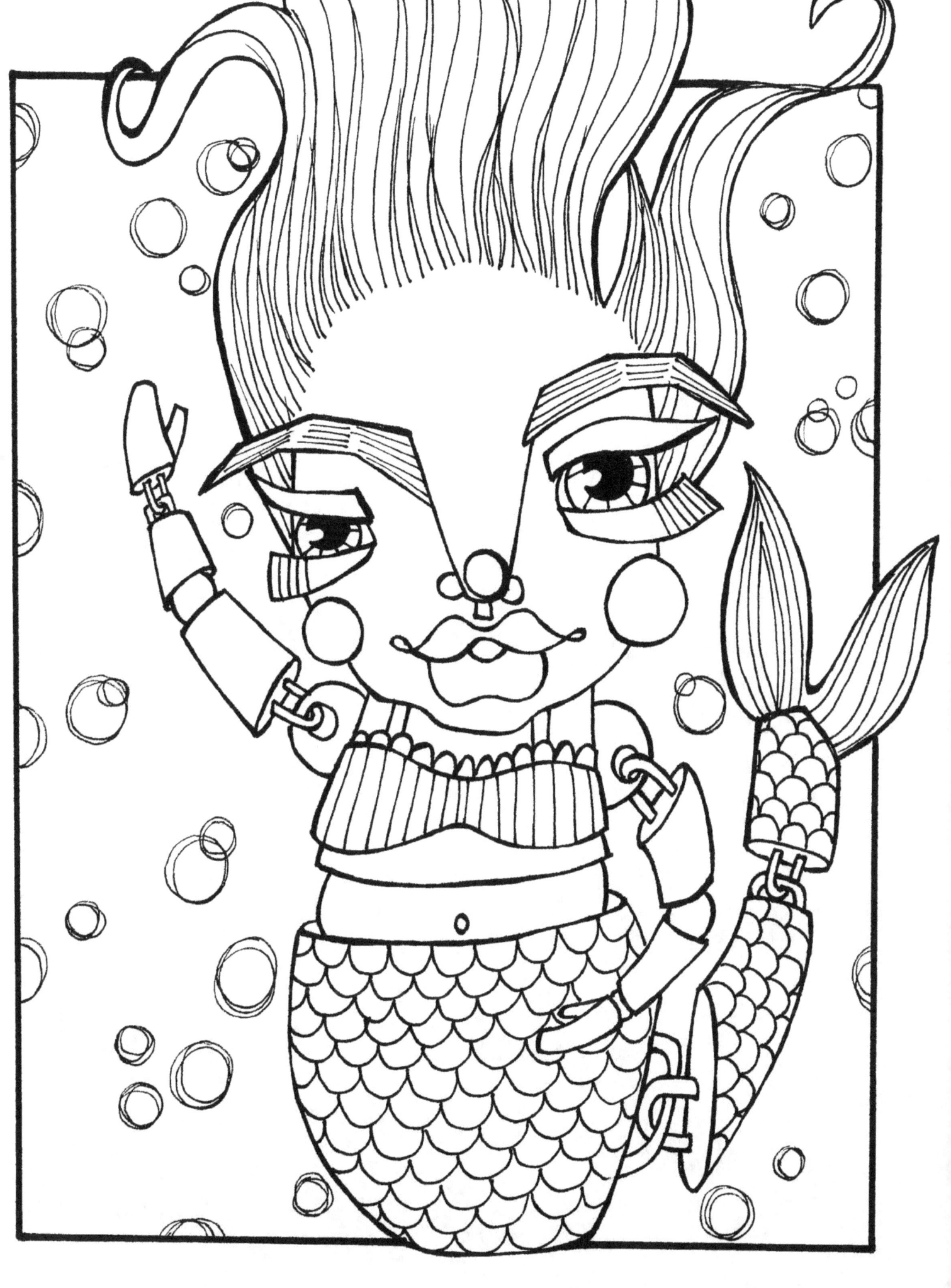

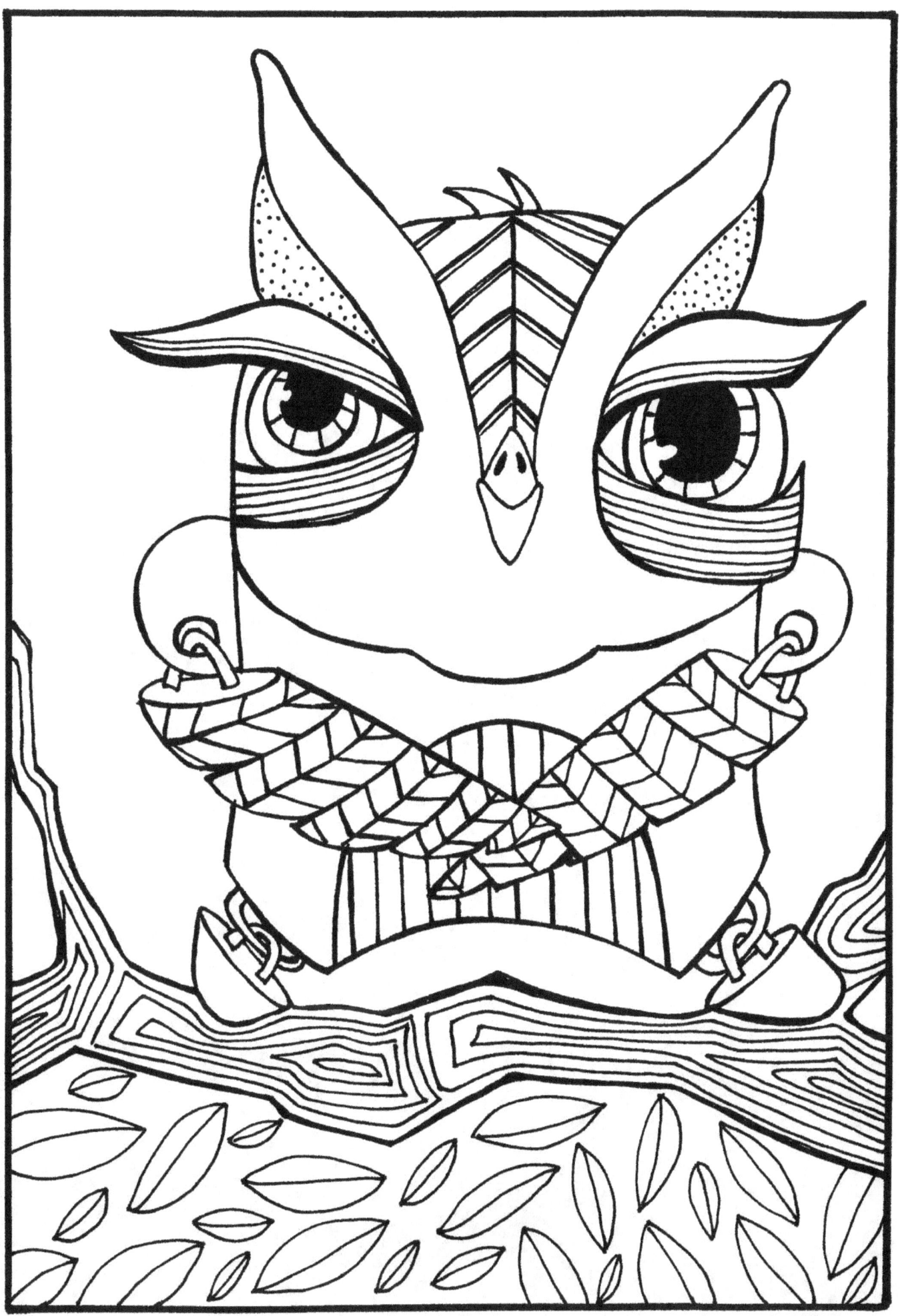

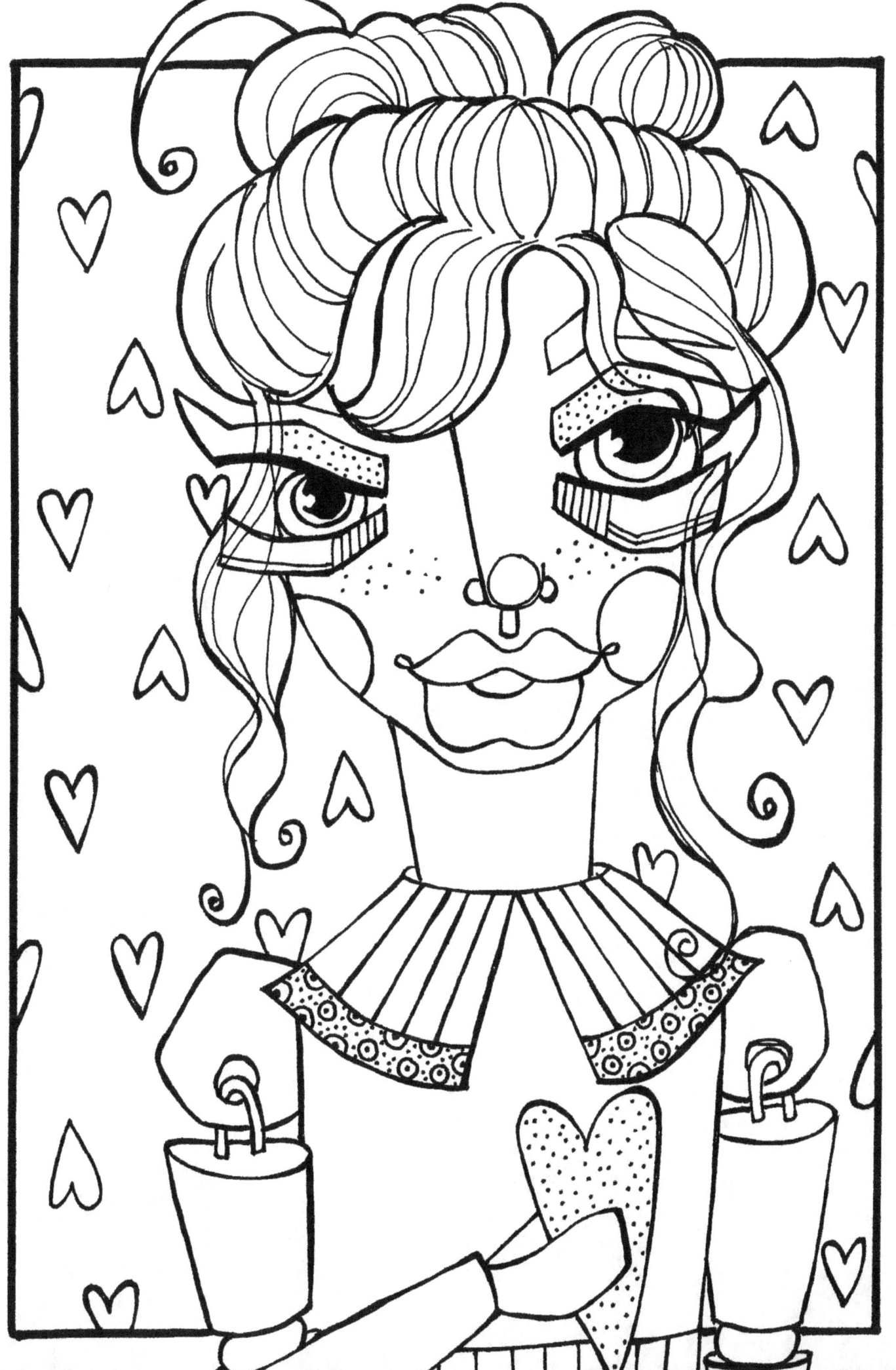

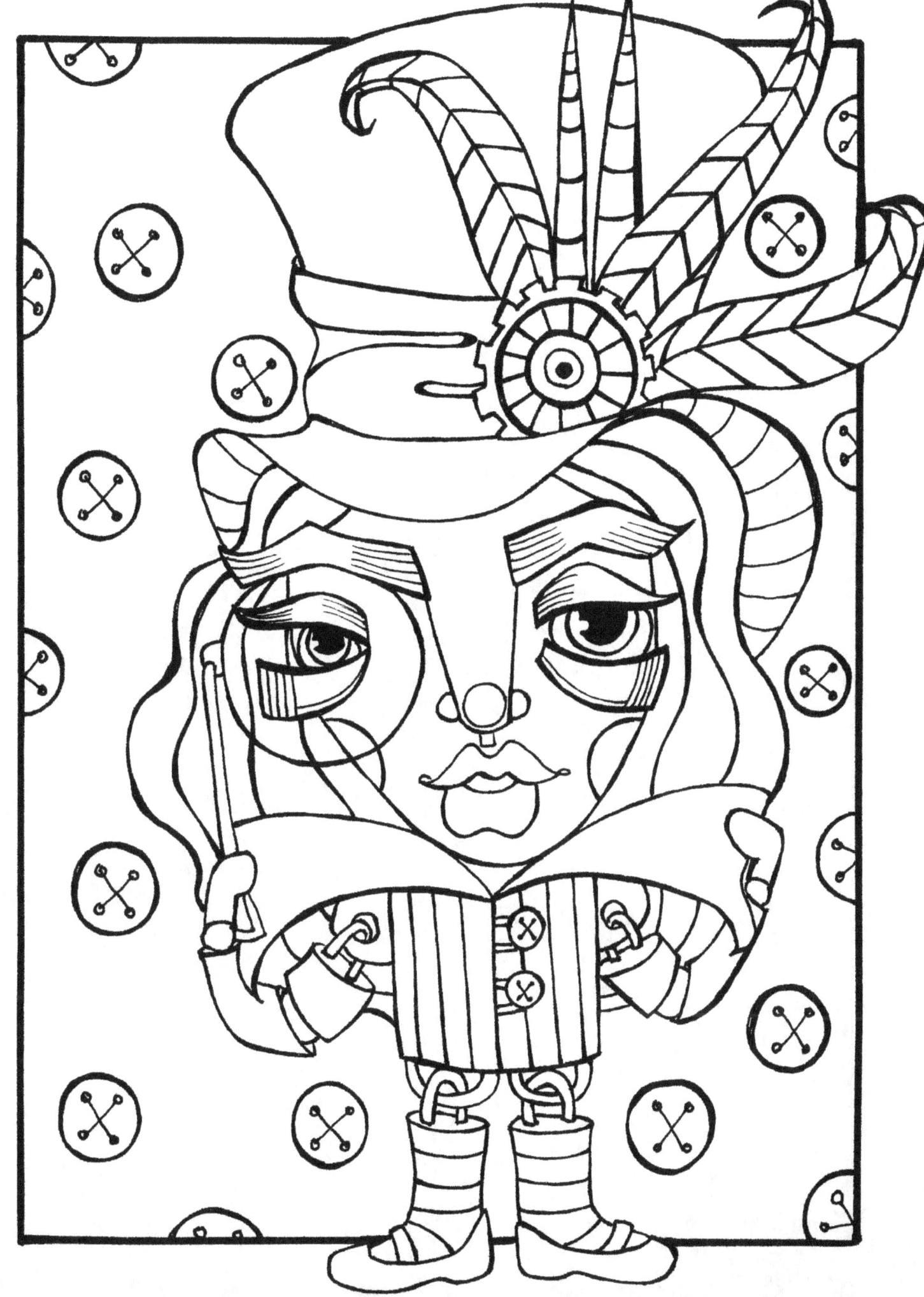